04-145

WITCH
HUNTERS

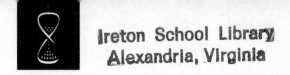
WITCH HUNTERS

PROFESSIONAL PRICKERS, UNWITCHERS &
WITCH FINDERS OF THE RENAISSANCE

P.G. Maxwell-Stuart

TEMPUS

First published 2003

Tempus Publishing Limited
The Mill, Brimscombe Port,
Stroud, Gloucestershire, GL5 2QG

British Library Cataloguing in Publication Data.
A catalogue record for this book is available from the British Library.

ISBN 0 7524 2339 8

Typesetting and origination by Tempus Publishing Limited
Printed in Great Britain by Midway Colour Print, Wiltshire

CONTENTS

INTRODUCTION

Identifying a witch is not easy. There is no in-born ability which sweeps one's friends and neighbours and whispers, 'That one is a witch'; and even those who did claim to be able to recognise witches at a glance relied, according to their own evidence, upon physical signs such as casts or defects in the eye, resembling a toad or a goat's foot, to alert them to the true nature of the person under scrutiny. Even if this led to an arrest, procedures had to be followed. Witnesses gave their statements, corroboration was needed, divergences were addressed, the accused was questioned, the final body of evidence was presented in a court of law, and a verdict and possibly sentence were then rendered. Identifying the witch's crime was not easy, either. For what was this 'witchcraft' with which she or he was to be charged? One can discern at least five very different kinds of activity which might be allowed to fall under this general heading: (a) diagnosing and curing illness in humans and animals; (b) deliberately causing illness and sometimes death in humans and animals, ruining crops or sinking ships and boats by manipulation of the weather, or causing accidents or other misfortunes; (c) worshipping Satan or some other demonic spirit either in private or in company with others during heretical, blasphemous assemblies; (d) causing evil spirits to take possession of another person to her or his pain and detriment; (e) predicting the future, finding hidden treasure or lost or stolen objects by revealing where they were and – sometimes – who had taken them. Since some of these activities were intended to be beneficial rather than malevolent, who decided what would be entered upon the charge-sheet levelled against a witch? Moreover, when one was interrogating a witch, was one supposed to take into account that the charge might have been brought maliciously by an ill-intentioned individual; or that the accused might be ill, or suffering from delusions, or willing to admit to anything because her or his immediate situation was frightening or intolerable? Guidance, in other words, was essential throughout the whole process of identifying, arresting, and then trying a witch, and the following chapters give an indication of whence that guidance might come, to whom it was addressed, and how well (or sometimes how badly) it seemed to work.

I

MARTÍN DEL RIO:
LAYING DOWN THE RULES

The usual starting point for those who wrote, often at length and very learnedly, about magic in general and witchcraft in particular was personal experience, sometimes obtained at first hand, sometimes at second. For Martín Del Rio, a Jesuit learned even by the standards of his Society, a second-hand experience came in 1597 when he stopped off at Liège on his way to take up a university post at Louvain. There he met, and probably stayed with, an old friend, the lawyer Pierre Dheure, who was then helping to investigate a bizarre and complex case of maleficent magic allied to witches' conventions and deaths by sorcery which had been uncovered in 1592 at the Benedictine abbey of Stavelot, some thirty or so miles south-east of Liège itself. Jean Del Vaulx, one of the abbey's monks, was deemed responsible for the deaths of seven of his brethren in a suspicious con-catenation of misfortune. Arrested, imprisoned and subjected to detailed questioning, Jean proved almost garrulously co-operative with the investigating committee: happy, for example, to tell his inquisitors how he and up to 200 others (whom he named) used to meet at such-and-such a place on such-and-such an occasion to par-ticipate in a witches' Sabbat. Pressed by his judges for more details, Del Vaulx produced the usual account of such a meeting, but with a number of interesting variants.

The Sabbat, he said, began with an adoration of Beelzebub (not Satan himself, but a demon of the first rank below him), who would appear in the form of a goat. Adoration done, Beelzebub then sat down at table with the evil spirit Leviathan on one side and a beautiful female demon, Astaroth, on the other, while everyone else was seated according to her or his rank in everyday society. After a feast of meat and alcohol, singing and dancing broke out spontaneously, fuelled by the drink and a sense of physical satisfaction; and then came the ritual sign to begin an orgy, kissing Beelzebub's anus, whereafter demons copulated with humans, and humans with other humans. Finally, sated by their experiences, the participants prepared to leave, but not before Beelzebub had given everyone powders which, when thrown into the air, would poison crops and raise destructive storms.

These details, along with many others, Pierre Dheure passed on to his friend Del Rio who reproduced them in the work for which he is most famous, *Investigations Into Magic*, a huge work on most of the occult sciences first published in three volumes in 1599 and 1600, which was to become one of the most influential guides for theologians, lawyers and physicians in Western Europe throughout the whole of the seventeenth century. How was he able to write so authoritative a work, and why did he choose to do so?

The 'how' becomes clear when we consider his remarkable education. Sent by his wealthy Spanish parents to colleges and universities in the Spanish Netherlands (then generally called 'Belgium'), France and Spain, he became fluent in nine languages including Latin (the lingua franca of intellectuals during this period), Greek, Hebrew, Chaldee, Flemish (the language of the region in which he was born), German, Spanish (his parents' tongue and therefore, presumably, the one he used at home), Italian and French. In Paris he studied the Classics, philosophy and mathematics; in Douai, philology; in Louvain, civil law, obtaining his bachelor's degree in 1570 at the age of nineteen; and in Salamanca he became a Doctor of Civil Law at the age of twenty-three. A year later, King Philip II made him a member of the governing council of Brabant, which meant he was back in 'Belgium', and there he carried out his duties so well that three years later the King appointed him Vice-Chancellor of the province and one of the Royal Treasury officials.

It was a dazzling career which promised to become yet more brilliant. But at the age of twenty-nine, Del Rio had other ideas, suddenly resigned all his posts, and retreated to Spain, ostensibly on vacation for the sake of his health; and there, on 9 May 1580, in Valladolid, he entered a Jesuit college and began the lengthy, rigorous spiritual and intellectual training required of a novice in the Society. So learned and well-experienced a man would obviously not take long to complete the necessary training, and it was quickly realised how much Del Rio could be an asset to the Society. So after five more years of study, he was appointed Professor of Theology at Douai, and from then until the end of his life the Society sent him to teach in various universities including Louvain, and Graz where he gained a second doctorate. It was a hard life of constant travel, study and teaching, and in the summer of 1608 his health began to fail. He was in Valladolid at the time and felt the need to return to finish some work in Louvain. But the long journey back by both land and sea drained the last of his strength from him and, when he finally reached Louvain on 18 October, it was clear he would not last long. The last rites were administered and at seven the following morning he died.

Why Del Rio chose to write extensively about magic is not so quickly answered. Like everyone else, of course, he came into frequent contact with it one way and another. While in Madrid in 1575, for example, he visited on more than one occasion a boy credited with the power to see objects hidden in the earth – one wonders why, and why he should have returned a second time and more: was he a client, or merely a curious onlooker? – he was once present in a civil court at the trial of two women whom he suspected of practising *veneficium*, a kind of magic involving poisonous substances; and he records that when he was an inquisitor in the province of Stavelot, he was convinced of the guilt of witches who had been jumping and dancing in a circle with such vigour that the man who played the pipes for them had collapsed exhausted on the ground. In Louvain he heard the story of a cobbler's wife from Brussels who used to foretell events with apparent accuracy with the help of a spirit-guide who manifested as a diffuse, white body without discernible features. From another informant he learned about a Westphalian werewolf who confessed to having made a pact with a demon to enable him to remain impervious to the pains of torture, no matter what people did to him; and from 'a devoutly religious man, well worthy of belief', he received the narrative of a barmaid who tried to cheat a customer by charging him double for his drinks, and when she was found out, threatened him: 'You will not have the power to reach your house today'. Sure enough, the man found he could not move his boat, not even with the help of some passing soldiers. Noticing a large toad at the bottom of the boat, however, one of the soldiers drilled a hole in the creature with his sword and threw it into the water, seemingly dead. Back at the inn, the barmaid was discovered dead in her room, wounded in just those places the soldier had stabbed the toad.

None of this renders Del Rio himself especially credulous. He records what he heard and saw and was told; and indeed he often gives evidence of personal doubt, as when, for example, he keeps an open mind about whether or not real gold can be produced by alchemy, or when he says that the son of a Count he knew used to pass large stones in his urine, a misfortune many people attributed to the maleficent magic of his Calvinist wife. Del Rio, however, observes that the stones could equally well have been due to purely natural causes. Del Rio was no narrow-minded bigot. But neither was he entirely sceptical. How could he be? He was a deeply religious man who accepted that the universe was full of non-human beings created, like humans, by God. He was also a very learned man whose extensive reading provided overwhelming testimonies of the reality of magicians, witches, demons, angels, and their whole repertoire of extraordinary achievements well beyond the capabilities of ordinary, unaided humans. He was also a man of his own times, not ours, and so responded to what he saw and read and was told in much the same way as any of his contemporaries in the complex, exciting and frightening world of post-Reformation Europe. That meant he saw and experienced a world torn by confessional wars of religion, with their attendant plagues and famines and cruelties; for although it was also a time of remarkable discoveries and re-discoveries by sailors on the one hand and intellectuals on the other, the immediacy of life in Western Europe conveyed to those who lived through it a sense of doom, a notion that the signs of the end of the world foretold in the *Apocalypse* were unmistakable to anyone who cared to look around him.

In Del Rio's eyes (as in those of so many of his Catholic contemporaries), Satan had been let loose to wreak havoc before the End, and he was busy recruiting helpers to aid him in his task. These helpers were witches and heretics. His homeland of 'Belgium', Del Rio said, was being devoured by a locust-swarm of Calvinists, Lutherans and Anabaptists. Magic and heresy (the two were companions-in-arms as far as he was concerned), were rampaging through the world like the ravening lion of 1 *Peter* 5.8, seeking whom they might devour. Magic was therefore not the idle superstition of ignorant peasants – undoubtedly not since, as he knew full well, both it and the other occult sciences were practised by every rank in society, as high as the Pope himself – but was instead humanity's Achilles heel, the principal means whereby Satan subverted human beings to aid him in his task of causing universal damnation and waging war upon God. Witches especially, since they were magical operators who had consciously allied themselves with the Devil, must be rooted out and extirpated. Only thus could society's health be restored and the End, if indeed it was coming, be faced with some degree of hopeful equanimity. Nor was Del Rio alone in this view. Protestants of all kinds by and large agreed, although they substituted 'the Catholic Church' for his 'heretics'; so we must therefore see the animus of churchmen, regardless of their confessional adherence, against witches and magic as an attempt to occupy high moral ground in the face of a tidal wave of Satanically inspired evil which was threatening to overwhelm and destroy humanity. The day of the final battle, it seemed to many, had arrived.

The reason for Del Rio's undertaking his immense exposition of magic is thus conjecturable. It was more necessary than ever for people to be alerted to the spiritual dangers which surrounded them and those who were entrusted with the spiritual and temporal governance of others must be the first to acquaint themselves with the nature of these perils and the remedies for them. Thus Del Rio's audience, as he tells us on his title page, consisted of scholars in general, but also theologians, 'jurisconsults' (by which he meant not simply experts in the law but practising advocates and judges), and physicians in particular, since these were the people most likely to be called on to deal with witches and magical workers in a professional capacity, and would welcome detailed guide-lines on the subject.

He begins by explaining what he means by 'superstition', which he sees as a form of worship, either superfluous to the norms laid down by the Church, or idolatrous, in as much as it steered the focus of people's attention away from God and thus towards some 'other'. All types of magic, he says, tend to fall into this latter category. Magic he divides into different but related types. These include 'natural', which meant that a magician could work apparent wonders by manipulating the hidden or secret laws and powers of nature; and 'artificial', by which he meant what we should call conjuring-tricks or illusions. The former might include curing diseases and treating wounds in ways other than purely medical, and since witches were frequently accused of working beneficent magic to precisely this end, one can see that even trying to do some apparent good might arouse suspicion, if it were being done in certain ways. Del Rio does recognise that artificial magic may be no more than legitimate entertainment *provided* (and here was the nub of the matter) the tricks were not done with the help of an evil spirit, but the very extraordinariness of such entertainment carried within it the seeds of uneasy doubt. He gives several examples,[1]

The following are things which (for shame!) certain very credulous, but otherwise pious princes allow to take place in their presence. Iron objects, silver platters, and similar things of great weight are put on top of a table and then, without the assistance of a magnet, a cord, a hair, or other means, are pulled from one end of the table to the other, jumping up and down as they go. Someone pulls out a playing-card from the rest of the pack without letting anyone else see it, and then its face is changed three times while the person still has the card in his hand. There are mirrors which seem to show things from far away places. In the space of three hours a real shrub is made to grow a span's length from the table, and trees with leaves and fruit suddenly appear. Lanterns lit with a special flame make all the women present look as though they are naked, and reveal those parts which nature tells us should remain concealed; and while the women are unclothed, they perform a ritual dance as long as a lantern, which is hung up in the middle of the room, continues to burn... Such things should be ascribed to trickery.

All this throws an interesting light on the variety and extent of the illusions which might be seen at noble and princely courts throughout Europe, and provides a useful reminder that educated people in earlier times – it is perhaps a little more difficult to come to an assessment about the mass of the uneducated, although these had their street and fair-ground entertainers – were perfectly well aware that stage-magicians were capable of dazzling their audiences by ingenious manipulations of one kind and another. Even so, meddling with people's perceptions had its drawbacks, as Del Rio indicates in another anecdote:

At Cologne, a young girl was summoned to appear in court. She had been performing remarkable things, apparently by magic, in front of an audience of the nobility. It was said she ripped a napkin to pieces and suddenly put it back together again in full view of everyone. She threw a glass at a wall. It broke and instantly she repaired it... She was excommunicated, but escaped the hands of the Inquisition.

Clearly the girl had been hired as an after-dinner divertissement, but someone among the spectators was disturbed enough to have the girl arrested and brought before the requisite authorities so that her talents could undergo detailed scrutiny by people sufficiently expert to be able to uncover any demonic help she might have been receiving; and enough suspicion must have lingered at the end of the examination to cause her to be excommunicated. But it seems she was not otherwise punished or seen to be tainted with heresy, which would certainly have landed her in serious trouble. Her situation as a professional illusionist was thus hazardous but not dangerous, an assessment which is more applicable to the majority of witches and other magical practitioners throughout most of Europe than one might think.

Their situation, to be sure, was somewhat different from hers. No one regarded them or hired them as entertainers. They offered their neighbours practical solutions to everyday problems, and whether they worked cures or wonders, their magic was likely to be regarded as a type generally known as 'demonic'. But most witches operated for years, even decades, in their communities, who consulted, used and paid for their peculiar skills, rather as though they were craftspeople along the lines of the local miller or blacksmith or midwife – specialists to whom one could turn when the occasion demanded. Still, the nature of the magic they practised was always liable to be viewed askance, especially by the Church, and in periods of particular tension there was always the possibility that the community might be swept by fear and so turn against those they had hitherto employed.

Demonic magic is the type which Del Rio discusses at length. It included such magical operations as the making of charms and amulets, uttering incantations for whatever purpose, necromancy and every kind of divination (so one can see how easily 'natural' and indeed 'artificial' magic might overlap with or merge into demonic) and, of course, all operations intended to inflict illness or harm or death upon humans, their crops and animals. Right from the start, Del Rio comes to two important conclusions which are to act as basic guides for anyone dealing with or affected by magic of any kind: (i) there is no such thing as 'white' magic, and (ii) all magical operations have as their foundation a pact made between the magical operator and an evil spirit. This is why *any* manifestation of magic is potentially harmful. Moreover, since evil spirits cannot be compelled by human beings to take part in such a pact (however much humans may delude themselves that this is possible), it follows that if they agree to co-operate, it is because they are pursuing their own agenda of unsparing hatred and see a means to damn the magician's soul and harm those foolish enough to make use of her or his services.

This pact involves the magical operator's renouncing his or her Christian faith, submitting to a fresh 'baptism' after which she or he is given a new name, and receiving the demon's mark. This is famously a place on the body, insensible to the pain of being pricked long and deep with a needle, and which emits no blood when so pierced. It is caused by the demon's grasping his new recruit, and is thus most frequently to be found on the neck, arm or shoulder. The unusual sarcoma or fold in the flesh, thought to be a teat wherefrom the witch fed her attendant spirit with her own blood, is not the same thing; and when witches were searched in their privy parts for evidence of their traffic with the Devil in animal form, it was this teat rather than a mark for which the searchers were looking.

Having submitted to Satan, the new witch might well give evidence of her or his changed allegiance by openly spurning the Christian religion in blasphemous word and sacrilegious deed. So anyone given to swearing and cursing, for example, even in drink, was laying him or herself open to suspicion. On the other hand, anyone who appeared to be excessively devout or who communicated rather frequently was equally liable to attract suspicious glances; for it was known that the Host, whether consecrated or not, was used in magical ceremonies. Some people, it was alleged, did not swallow the Host when the priest put it on their tongue, but carried it home and misused it nefariously. Too great or too little devotion in someone accused might therefore be signs that a priest or a judge would do well to bear in mind if neighbours commented on it in giving evidence.

But the priest and the judge would also need to remember that the pact with an evil spirit might be implicit as well as explicit. Del Rio explains this as meaning that either 'someone knowingly and willingly uses those superstitious signs [i.e. instruments] usually employed by magicians, which he gets either from books or from conversations with magicians or other people', or that 'someone unknowingly uses magical signs because he does not know they are evil and originate from an evil spirit'. We can see an example of this latter implicit pact in the Scottish case of Janet MacPatrick who, in November 1653, explained to the presbytery session of Forres that she had given charms to various women, having learned the method from her father. She saw no harm in it and wondered why the presbytery was wasting its time on her. The ministers 'finding her to be a mere ignorant, informed her what danger there was in charming', and although their terms of explanation would not have been quite the same as Del Rio's (they being Presbyterian and he a Catholic), their basic perceptions of her wrong-doing would not have been all that different. Dabbling with magic, even if done out of ignorance, was still trafficking with the Devil and therefore condemnable and dangerous for all concerned.

We have already seen that Del Rio, partly under the influence of Jean Del Vaulx's description of a witches' Sabbat, produced a fairly detailed account for his readers. He also dealt with the vexed question of how witches got there, and whether they really flew through the air or were deluded by drugs or illness or Satanic fantasies into imagining they had done so. Catholic and Protestant writers alike were divided on the subject. Del Rio summarises the copious arguments on both sides and comes to the conclusion that both opinions may be correct, for while it is perfectly possible that a witch may be deluded, the fact that she *can* be does not mean she always *is*. Nor does he neglect common sense: 'If they live nearby, they go on foot', he says. (Compare Agnes Sampson who, in 1589, made her way to a witches' convention in North Berwick from her home in Nether Keith, a distance of perhaps twenty miles or so, travelling on horseback with her son-in-law.)

Nevertheless, Del Rio is nothing if not logical. Given the premise of a universe created and ruled by God and the presence therein of non-human entities, some of which are good and others evil, the preternatural explanation for witches' flight cannot be dismissed or underestimated; and so by and large he favours the reality of the experience. When witches anoint themselves, he says, and say they are transported, it is no figment of their imagination. They take careful note of their surroundings, unless they are masked, and of what they do and whom they meet. They are often seen by other, perfectly sane,

Catholics, going to and returning from their meetings. Sometimes they have been seen and arrested without any clothes on, or they may have fallen from the sky, or they have been badly wounded. When the witches get home, they are so tired they sleep for three days. They all confess the same thing with corroborative details, and their flight owes nothing to any medical condition or to dreams – and here one can envisage the theologians and lawyers reading this passage and nodding their heads in agreement. Their experience in both court-room and confessional bore witness to the truth of what Del Rio was saying. Over and over again, accused persons told the same story, while reliable witnesses confirmed even the most extraordinary details; and in a world over-run by demons and alien spirits, why should they not be true?

On the one hand, there is no reason at all why such things should not be true, and yet although it may be perfectly possible for Satan to transport people through the air, anyone who may be watching the individual witch as she makes her journey thither may see no actual movement, no disappearance, but only a person who seems to be fast asleep. (About a hundred and fifty years before Del Rio, the Dominican friar Johannes Nider recorded the observation of wit-nesses, perhaps including himself, to a witch's preparation for flight to a Sabbat. In their presence, the woman smeared herself with ointment, recited some magic formulae, and then fell asleep; and yet when she awoke after a long time, she maintained she had indeed flown to her meeting.) Such discrepancies were very well known and widely debated. But Del Rio sounds a note of caution.

It is the Devil's habit to deceive in a number of different ways. Sometimes, for example, he substitutes one body for another. He puts a person to sleep and while he or she is off in some secret place, he takes the body of a wolf or manufactures one out of air, and wraps himself in it, like a garment. Consequently people believe that the things he does are done by the poor wretch who is actually some-where else, fast asleep.

This may account for the shape-changing often associated with witches, and certainly explains why married women were apparently able to leave their beds for hours at a time without their husband's noticing. The Devil had left a replica of the wife next to the man. 'Evil spirits', Del Rio warned, 'can construct for themselves from air and from the other elements bodies which feel like flesh to the touch. These they can move as they wish and make them warm' – an ability which also explains how *incubi* and *succubae*, spirits who look like men and women, are able to have sexual intercourse with human beings, a capability they do not, as immaterial entities, possess otherwise.

Del Rio thus takes into account one of the most potent features of the Middle Ages and early modern world, the ever-present sense that there is more than one universe lurking behind the outward appearance of this material world, which are liable in an instant to slip through the flimsy veil which separates them and impinge upon physical life. We should not misunderstand this open-mindedness. It is not that, when faced by apparent evidences of such intrusions, Del Rio automatically plumps for the preternatural explanation every time. (A werewolf, he says, for example, 'may be suffering from a fault in the humours and an excess of black bile, which has caused their mind to be taken over by a kind of wolfishness': in other words, they have a medical and psychological problem.) But he conscientiously lays out for the benefit of his readers the full range of possibilities they ought to consider when dealing with magical operators, and with witches in particular; and he sometimes makes personal choices from this range, telling his readers why he thinks one explanation for a phenomenon is likely to be more credible than another.

In Book 3 of his *Investigations*, Del Rio devotes a great deal of space to describing acts of specifically maleficent magic which operators of harmful magic (usually witches) may let loose upon others. They use powders which they mix in food or drink, rub on bare flesh or scatter over clothes. Herbs, pieces of straw, and ointments are part of their armoury; they poison people merely by breathing or blowing on them; even sacred objects such as a holy water sprinkler may be subverted to their evil purposes. All this is *veneficium*: 'poisonous magic'.

Witches kill small children and babies in various ways, quite often by smothering them while they sleep. Their very glance is lethal – the technical term for such a baleful enchantment, by the way, is 'fascination' – and people must beware of anyone who approaches their newly born child and praises it, for what appears to be a kindly act may conceal a malevolent intention. Hence the custom, inherited from the ancient world, of hanging an amulet of some kind round the child's neck in order to protect it from the evil eye. Witches abort children from the womb, dry up nurses' (and cows') milk, and cause a great variety of illnesses both physical and psychological, including those during which the patient vomits up solid objects such as thorns, bones, pebbles, pieces of glass, needles and knives. They send evil spirits to occupy people's bodies and so make them blaspheme and deny God, rave at the sight and touch of holy objects, and distort themselves physically in ways not otherwise natural or possible. They tie knots in a cord and thereby render men impotent; they set houses on fire – the list of their misdeeds is almost endless. In a word, however, they corrupt, maim and kill, and all, apparently, out of nothing more than a desire to gratify their own feelings of personal malice and hatred.

Now comes the great question: why? Why does God allow workers of harmful magic to run riot in tandem with Satan and evil spirits? There are various reasons, says Del Rio. If humans suffer malefices, then God's clemency, wisdom, power and justice are more forcefully demonstrated, since the innocent are tested, like Job, and have the chance to prove their faith, after which they will receive appropriate reward; sinners will be punished in this life and so be given an opportunity to repent before they die; the truth of the Catholic faith is asserted against those who try to say there are neither angels nor demons; God's dominion over the Devil is shown time and again, to the comfort of all human beings, whether they are suffering from Satan's especial hostility or not; and the Devil's secret helpers are revealed, since faithful Christians do not resort to magic in any form. The world, then, is being tested. The innocent will survive unscathed, their constancy strengthened, while the guilty will be discovered and afterwards punished, either by human or divine justice.

A volume devoted to the complex business of foretelling the future follows. Some methods, such as prophecy, Del Rio regards as perfectly licit. Others, however, such as divination, are not because they depend upon the assistance of an evil spirit who, of course, will co-operate with a human only if the human has entered into some kind of pact with him. Every branch of divination falls under this condemnation; one cannot use water, fire, stones, rods, the flight of birds, the lines on the hand or face – even astrology is suspect, although Del Rio makes certain reservations to accommodate predictions made from the purely mathematical mechanics of the art. Almanacs, therefore, are acceptable because they merely show the predicted positions of heavenly bodies for every day during a given period. Astrology which predicts that a future event is *bound* to happen, however, is superstitious and illicit, and Del Rio looks askance at medical astrology because it so often makes just this kind of confident prediction:

> Those physicians who make diagnoses according to the position of the moon and the other planets in the signs of the zodiac [e.g. which sickness will happen to someone, and which arrangements of stars will enable a cure to be found], even if they are not superstitious are certainly harmful to the patients. So are surgeons who examine wounds in the same way and take into account the day on which the wound was made and the stars which preside over them... and thus pronounce the wound either mortal or curable.

Testing a person's guilt or innocence may also fall into this dubious area of divination, and Del Rio picks out a familiar and widespread method for discovering whether or not someone is a witch:

> Today, in many places in Germany, and especially the area round Westphalia, they use this proof to track down workers of harmful magic. These people are regarded as suspicious because of their reputation or because they have been denounced by other women. Then straight away, without further investigation, they are arrested, brought out of the city where their right hand is tied to their left foot and their

left hand to their right foot, and thrown into cold water. If the women float, they are very strongly suspected of beings workers of poisonous magic and are thereupon subjected to severer questioning. But if they sink, they are believed to be innocent.

This Del Rio thinks is both illicit and sinful on the grounds that practice has actually been forbidden by canon law and Papal decree, it smacks of testing God, and it is open to the suspicion that the accused person is being assisted by an evil spirit, so that the judge who authorises this test runs the risk of colluding in a demonic pact. There are other, legitimate means of ascertaining the truth, and these are the ones to use. In the end, Del Rio remarks, it is better to let a guilty person go free than to find her or him guilty by indications which are not legally admissible.

So now, having completed a detailed guide to what witches and other magical operators do, why and how they do it, and why they are allowed to do it, Del Rio presents the last two volumes of his work, in which he offers advice and observation first to lawyers, and finally to confessors.

It was a common idea that judges had to be careful when trying witches, for the power of their evil eye might affect the court's ability to hear the case impartially. Del Rio records this belief but regards it as nonsense ('childish drivel' is his actual phrase), and notes that God will protect those judges who proceed according to proper form and in accordance with justice, an opinion which was widely held by others but which also reflects his own wish to see everything in such cases done with complete probity. He describes the great care which must be taken at every stage of the proceedings. For example, since witchcraft is an offence pertaining both to religion, through its association with evil spirits and defiance of God, and to secular affairs through its destruction of crops and animals or the murder of innocent people, the judge himself should be equally learned in canon and civil law. Apart from cases of divination and malefice where heresy is not involved, there should be no time-limit on the period for investigation; and in all cases of witchcraft a person may be investigated in her or his absence, because the crime is so grave that the normal objection to this which one finds in civil law cannot be allowed to stand. But the character of the evidence against an accused, too, must be scrutinised from every angle. Malice in such matters is always possible and therefore princes ought to be careful how they issue orders to have someone investigated, since accusers can often take advantage of princes' natural goodness and credulity. So the accused must be notorious as a witch, or the object of common gossip to that effect.

Del Rio constantly refers to 'investigation'. This is because he is thinking in terms of Roman law which requires that a competent judge make detailed inquiries into an accusation and thereby accumulate the written dossier which will form the basis of a possible later trial. What he is investigating is denunciation, circumstantial evidence, and direct information taken from the accused. Denunciation, as we have seen, may be tainted because of malice. But even if it comes from someone who claims to have been an accomplice or fellow-witch (and many such denunciations were made during the course of witch-investigations – sometimes made freely, sometimes under duress), Del Rio reminds us that the source is unreliable because by its nature it is disreputable. He therefore recommends that the accomplice's evidence be treated with the utmost caution to eliminate the possibility of rancour; the accomplice's character must be taken into account; he or she must be questioned closely about the circumstances in which the accused was observed to commit the offence with which she or he is being charged; and if necessary, the denunciator should be tortured to verify what he or she is alleging. Denouncing someone as a witch thus carried its own hazards, and if Del Rio's recommendations were followed, only a serious accusation would be able to penetrate the surrounding legal safeguards.

Circumstantial evidence (*indicia*) he divides into slight, serious and very serious. Slight *indicia* gave rise merely to suspicion. Shedding tears while one is being tortured is one such, and is clearly related to the widespread belief that a witch is unable to cry at all. Del Rio, however, dismisses this notion as frivolous: 'I have known children you could flog till they bled, but you could not shake a single tear out of them'. Serious *indicia* give rise to more than suspicion but less than proof. Running away before an investigation has been instituted or an accusation levelled might constitute such a piece of evidence, although again the judge must be careful to ascertain precisely why the person ran away. Had he received a judicial summons to appear in court? Was he discovered in the process of committing an offence, or preparing to do so, and rendered fugitive by a subsequent hue and cry? Was he afraid he might be arrested and thrown into prison? Had he fled into deep, wild country – a possible indication that he wanted to avoid people and thus recognition or arrest? Finally, very serious *indicia*. Del Rio tells a story to illustrate this type,

> In the town of Halle in the diocese of Utrecht, a wretched woman one day put her feet in a basin and then jumped out of it, saying, 'Here I jump from the power of God into the power of the Devil'. The Devil snatched her away and bore her up in the air in the sight of many people who were inside the house and out, carrying her over the tops of forests; and to this day no one has caught even a glimpse of her. Johann Caesarius has clearly shown that this was done by magic arts. Certainly I should think that a word or deed of this kind would be a most compelling indication and one which would touch the suspect very closely.

Once the judicial investigation is complete and all the gathered evidence has been committed to paper, then (and only then) can the suspect be arrested. During the arrest, 'all the floors and corners of the house must be searched thoroughly at once in case there should be found little boxes, ointments, powders, and other instruments of malefice. Defendants ought not to be allowed to return to the house in case they take drugs which will assist them to remain silent'. (For similar reasons, Del Rio later says, the defendant must be stripped and searched before torture, to ascertain whether or not she or he has concealed in or about her person or clothing amulets or some other magical devices which will provide protection from pain and damage.) Imprisonment after arrest, however, does not relax Satan's power over such people because, in spite of opinion to the contrary, it is well-known that witches can and do continue to inflict magical damage to people and crops even from their prison cell. For Satan has access to them, and it has been noticed that he may have sexual intercourse with them, or do physical harm to them, or persuade them to despair of their condition and kill themselves. Consequently, Del Rio urges, the suspect should be brought to trial as quickly as possible after arrest and imprisonment.

Witchcraft, however, was a difficult crime to prove, since the malefice was essentially a secret act committed by the witch in league with an evil spirit. Sometimes she or he operated in full view of others, but generally the evidence of witnesses related to circumstantial *indicia* rather than direct observation. 'I quarrelled with X. X left me, voicing threats. A certain time afterwards, my child fell sick and died. This must be witchcraft because X has long had a reputation for being a witch'. Confession, on the other hand, provided irrefutable proof of the crime, and therefore every effort was made to bring the suspect to confession. These efforts included verbal exhortation, trickery and torture. But Del Rio is clear that a judge should refrain from using torture if he can get at the truth some other way, because torture often produces unreliable results.

Now, it is not as widely appreciated as it should be that torture was not applied to suspects willy nilly according to the caprice of individual judges or inquisitors. Roman law prescribed rules for its use, and if those rules were too frequently bent or ignored, these breaches of the law do not nullify the fact that such rules existed, and Del Rio repeats and affirms them for the better information and guidance of his readers. For example, the accused should never be tortured more than three times for any reason, and the torture must not be repeated on the same day; novel forms of torture must not be devised; if the suspect denies in court the next day what she confessed under torture previously, she may be tortured again: but if she denies her confession a second time, all process of torture must cease. This meant, of course, that a confession obtained under torture had to be ratified at least twenty-four hours later without torture, otherwise it was invalid and could not be tested again.

Finally come judgement and sentence. Quite frequently, defendants were acquitted and Del Rio distinguishes between a definitive acquittal which meant that an accused had been found completely innocent because he or she did not commit the crime, and provisional acquittal which did not indicate 'innocent', but 'not guilty' because on this occasion the evidence presented to the court had not been sufficient for a conviction. But even a confession might not be enough to have a defendant declared guilty, for part of the judge's duty was to consider whether the confession was real or merely idle. In other words, had the accused confessed to actions which really had happened, or had she or he confessed to fantasies (whether caused by illness or diabolical delusion) in the belief they were real? That decided, if the verdict turned out to be guilty, what should the sentence be? Suppose, for example, the culprit were a priest who had celebrated Mass over objects which were then used for magical purposes; the appropriate punishment would consist of his being degraded from his priestly status and being subject to a five-year term of penance. Or what of someone who had consulted a magician or diviner? She or he would be liable either to deportation and exile, or to execution according to the discretion of the judge and the provisions of the specific law-code under which the defendant was tried.

In the case of witches, however, Del Rio entertained no doubt.

> Witches should be killed whether they have murdered anyone with a magical herb or poison, or not: and whether they have done harm to crops or living creatures, or not. Even if they have not practised necromancy, the very fact that they allied themselves with an evil spirit by means of a pact, that they were accustomed to take part in a Sabbat, and are responsible for what they do there, is sufficient reason.

It is an opinion entirely consistent with that view of witchcraft with which he had opened his advice to lawyers.

> It is a crime of great enormity, great seriousness, and great wickedness because in it are combined the particular circumstances of outrageous

crimes – apostasy, heresy, sacrilege, blasphemy, murder, and not infre-
quently parricide, unnatural sexual intercourse with a spiritual creature, and hatred of God; and there can be no offences more dreadful
than these.

Del Rio closes with advice to confessors, including these in his survey
because they act in a dual capacity, that of judge and physician; for
when they hear the sins of those who confess to employing magic or
divination, they sit in judgement upon acts which may well be unlaw-
ful according to divine as well as secular law, and they offer advice to
the penitent to help him or her cure a spiritual sickness and administer
remedies for their diseased condition. It is notable, therefore, that in
this, his final volume, Del Rio devotes most of his space to discussing
the various ways in which situations and conditions caused by magic
either should or should not be set right. Thus, it is illicit, he says, to
seek help from one magical practitioner to undo a malefice caused by
another. On the other hand, it is permissible to use natural remedies to
counteract the effects of harmful magic; and so one may employ herbs
to expel poison which has been introduced into the body via some
instrument of malefice, or to drive out evil spirits who have buried
themselves inside a person through a similar agency. Del Rio discusses
this last at some length, leaning especially upon two authors: an Italian
physician, Giovanni Battista Codronchi; and an Italian exorcist,
Zacharias Visconti.

> Some of those who have been subjected to malefice have complex-
> ions the colour of cedar wood. In other cases, their eyes are con-
> tracted, all parts of their body seem to be stiff, and their shoulders are
> dry to the touch. But there are two very powerful signs: constriction
> of the heart and constriction of the entrance to the stomach, espe-
> cially when they imagine they have some kind of cyst or ulcer above
> the stomach. Some have stabbing pains in the heart, as though it had
> been pierced with pins. Some imagine their heart is being gnawed
> away. Some have a great pain in the heart or in the kidneys and think
> that dogs are tearing at these parts of their body. Some imagine there

is a bolus rising and falling in their throat. Certain of them think their channel of generation has been tied off. Some have their stomach so disposed that they vomit whatever they eat or drink.

It is an account which appears to derive from a medical writer; in fact, it comes from Visconti's *Complete Account of the Art of Exorcism*, and serves to remind us that Del Rio was writing for a mixed readership of theologians, lawyers and doctors. Each profession needed to know the thinking of the others in regard to magic as a whole and witchcraft in particular, and here Del Rio is making sure that confessors realise they must not only be on the look-out for physical symptoms of possession or bewitchment, but that they need to be able to distinguish these from signs of an illness arising from natural, not magical, causes. They should also, he says, warn their penitents against charlatans who claim to be able to exorcise evil spirits from persons or places by the use of formulae and ceremonies which differ from those authorised by the Church; or who boast they can drive away unwanted clouds or 'cater-pillars, locusts, beetles, and other insects and vermin which feed on fruit, roots and seeds, and frustrate the farmers' hopes'. The Church provides people with all the help they require to sustain and repel the attacks of Satan and his confederates, both human and demonic, so there is no need for anyone to seek assistance from any other source; and thus, with a final blast against superstition, Del Rio ends his work.

Del Rio ends as he began, with references to disease and destruction of crops. They are themes which run throughout the *Investigations*, as he examines the vast range of magical activities employed in both good and bad faith by the society of his time. Magic and therefore witchcraft, he says in his initial dedicatory letter to Prince-Archbishop Ernst of Bavaria, a man interested in all the occult sciences, is a plague which has spread itself through the whole world in a very short space of time. 'Plague' is a metaphor he repeats over and over again, along with references to loss of crops and violent death by poison: just those activities which were thought to mark out a witch from other magical practitioners, and which together suggested a common image, that of a frightening, lingering death. What Del Rio offers his readers in the face of all this is warning and comfort. This is how bad things are, he seems to be saying, but remedies do exist – not the remedies suggested to you by workers of magic (do not turn to them, however innocent or well-intentioned they may seem to be: they are all in one way or another snares set for you by Satan), but the remedies offered by the Church. These alone are both licit and effective.

Investigations is thus a deeply religious work, although it is perhaps the breadth of its treatment that made it an instant publishing success. Del Rio, like his predecessors and contemporaries, and unlike us, does not draw clear distinctions between the various occult subjects he is discussing. We tend to treat witchcraft as though it were separate from the rest of magic, and worry about its exact relationship with religion and what we now call 'science'. For the Middle Ages and the early modern period, however, magic was magic and spanned a very wide spectrum, and therefore the difference we often like to perceive between well-intentioned magic and malefice did not exist for them. Consequently 'witch' was a term very hard to define exactly, since a witch might be a person living in a community exactly as her neighbours lived, sometimes quarrelling over trifles, sometimes not, but who was consulted from time to time for her (or his) special skill, whatever that happened to be. Suggest, as Del Rio and his contemporaries did, that *all* magical activity *might* depend on a pact with an evil spirit, and it is not surprising either that the precise nature of an individual act could be difficult to gauge, or that there might be no perceived difference between a well-intentioned act and an ill one.

In this, as in much else, Del Rio offers his readers no new theories. But this was not his intention. What he does, and intended to do, is to bring together everything concerning all the occult sciences, but especially magic and witchcraft, which had been discussed before by others, both pro and contra, and place it lucidly in front of his public along with informed and intelligent comment. This he does brilliantly, and it is therefore no surprise that *Investigations* rapidly became the principal reference work on the subject for both Catholics and Protestants, and remained so until well into the eighteenth century. Moreover, the work is immensely readable. This is at least in part due to the abundance of telling anecdotes with which he illustrates his themes. Noteworthy in particular are those he takes from the reports of contemporary Jesuit missionaries as far afield as Peru in the west and Japan in the east, for these emphasise the universality of Satan's machinations and the success of the Church's resistance, and so comfort while they divert and frighten his readership. Above all, perhaps, Del Rio gives the deserved impression of being master of his complex subject, and thus earns his readers' confidence, providing them with a sure guide to the workings, the traps and illusions which informed that bewildering nexus of interpenetrating worlds which both he and they inhabited.

2

PIERRE DE LANCRE:
WHO WILL GUARD THE GUARDS?

To the question, 'Did witches really exist and was their witchcraft real?'
the only practical answer for an historian is 'Yes'. From the ancient
world to the threshold of modern times in the eighteenth century,
people all over the western hemisphere took for granted the presence
among them of witches, magicians, sorcerers, diviners, cunning folk –
all practisers of magic in some kind – and accepted both them and the
validity of their crafts with the same combination of belief and cer-
tainty their twenty-first-century descendants bring to their contem-
plation of and functioning within the world. Scholars might theorise a
few express reservations about certain aspects of magical, astrological
or alchemical operations, but their treatises attempt to explain (largely
to each other, since most people could not read Latin) the *realities* of a
universe in which the laws responsible for preternatural phenomena
were as real to them as those of atomic structure are to us, and the consequences of an individual's manipulation of those laws were real as
well. There is thus no point in our approaching these earlier times with
sceptical apostrophes at the ready, as though our doubts on the subject
will make any difference to our ancestors, and if we wish to understand
why they acted as they did, we shall have to grant the sincerity of their
acceptance of a universe operating in accordance with rules quite different from those we are prepared to acknowledge.

With this necessary disjunction granted, we may approach Pierre de Lancre, a sixteenth-century French lawyer, who acquired a reputation for both credulousness and savagery in his role as investigating magistrate during a major outbreak of witchcraft in the Pays de Labourd, a Basque-speaking region of south-west France, in 1609. In a lengthy account of his experiences that year, he gives three rules or pieces of guidance to assist anyone who wishes or needs to be able to recognise truth from fiction when it comes to witchcraft. He wrote,

The confessions of male and female witches [*sorciers*][2] are in agreement with *indicia* so strong that one can maintain they are genuine, real, and neither deceptive nor illusory. This relieves judges of any misgiving they may have. For when they [the witches] confess to infanticide, parents find their children have been suffocated or their blood completely sucked out of them. When they confess to digging up corpses and violating the sacred nature of graves, one discovers that bodies have been torn from their graves and are no longer found where they had been put. When they confess they have given a piece of their clothing to Satan as a pledge, one finds this tell-tale scrap upon their person. When they say they have cast evil on such and such a person or animal, (and sometimes they confess they have cured them), it is self-evident they have been subject to malefice, they have been wounded, or they have been cured. Consequently, this is not an illusion. Here is the first rule which makes us see clearly what the witch has done, either through her confession strengthened by compelling *indicia* and very great, very strong presumptions, or by irreproachable witnesses.

The second rule whereby one may recognise them is to know if Satan can do what they confess, or what the witnesses testify against them. Now... transvection and everything else of which they are accused is not only possible for him, but very easy.

The third rule is derived from the character and great number of witnesses, and from the infinite number of witches cured and rescued by the grace of God and the intercessions of the Church, and who say as much forcefully and without guile to those who have not been rescued: five hundred children from Labourd, indeed more than a thousand (even though this is only a small region), who are taken every day to witches' meetings by these wicked women, who are all given the mark and carry the stamp of the Devil; and almost as many who sleep every night in the church, very much safer than those who, if they sleep one night outside, fall back into the Devil's clutches by means of the witch who usually took them to the Sabbat; events which agree with one another, a notable harmony of various things which are different from one another, and the universal agreement of every nation however distant they may be from one another that [witches] do narrate and describe the same things. If these were dreams, how did they, or could they, have the same dream? How is it possible that it happened to them in the same way, in the same place, at the same time, on the same day, at the same hour? Physicians say that the amount and quality of what people eat make dreams different, as do diversity in their ages, and the difference in the temperature of their humours. Nevertheless, when it comes to witchcraft, they dream the same thing, whether they be small or big, old or young, men or women, bilious or phlegmatic, sanguine or melancholic!

(*Tableau* Book 6, discourse 5, section 5).

The points De Lancre is making here are interesting. His argument that circumstantial evidence supports the details of witches' confessions is neither new nor peculiar to himself – it was a standard observation among most writers on the subject – but his choice of illustrative examples is noteworthy. Infanticide by suffocation or vampirism points on the one hand to a common cause of death which criminal courts might well be prepared to treat as a kind of manslaughter, since it was known that parents sometimes inadvertently killed their children by rolling on top of them during sleep; while on the other, the witch as night-hag who feeds on children's blood is a much more complex figure. Witches, we are told by Heinrich Institoris, were in the habit of eating babies, and he gives an example told to him by the inquisitor of Como. The inquisitor had been called in to investigate the death of a child. Its father had discovered it was missing from its cradle, and apparently had then seen a group of women kill the child, drink its blood, and then eat its flesh, (*Malleus Maleficarum* Part I, question II). Bartolommeo de Spina gives further details. In order to be able to suck children's blood, he says, witches scratch open the children's veins with a finger-nail or a needle, or receive help from an evil spirit. These wounds leave small scars, and sometimes, when the witches have taken the form of cats, one can see drops of blood near the shrieking children after the cats have fled (*De strigibus* question 8).

To us this may sound like wild fantasy. But what are we to make of an observation by the nineteenth-century physician Giovanni Alonzi, that Sicilian peasant women expressed their love for their children by kissing them violently and biting them and sucking their blood until the child cried out in pain; and if the child had done wrong, the women would not only strike it, but would bite it on the face, the ears or the arms until the blood began to flow? In the light of such behaviour, the alleged actions of vampiric witches begin to look slightly less like extravagant fiction, and a little more like exaggerated (and somewhat Gothic) reportage based on either some kind of real social and cultural phenomena, or upon folk memory thereof. But it is also worth remembering that one of the Latin words for a witch, *strix*, was derived from a Greek word meaning 'owl', and that in Classical times these birds had an evil reputation. 'They fly at night', says Ovid, 'seeking children without a nurse, and despoil their bodies after snatching them from their cradles. They are said to pluck the entrails out of the sucklings with their beaks, and their throats are filled with the blood they drink' (*Fasti* 6.135–8). The use of Latin by learned commentators therefore played a significant role in perpetuating certain word-associations, associations which are lost if the Latin is translated only as 'witch'.

As for the piece of cloth given in pledge to Satan, suspect witches were usually searched, not only for the mark Satan had left on their body as a sign of his ownership, but also for any amulets which might enable them to withstand torture without feeling the pain. As Del Rio observed, Satan 'usually furnishes them with pieces of parchment and other instruments of magic, on which are written various characters.

These are concealed in the most private parts of the body and, in accordance with the [diabolic] pact, remove the sense of pain' (*Disquisitiones Magicae* Book 5, section 9). Sometimes this amulet took the form of a piece of cloth. When a witch was bound to the stake in St Andrews in April 1572 ready to be garrotted, she was searched by the Provost who found between her legs a white cloth like a neckerchief, with knotted strings attached. He removed it, and at once the condemned woman cried out that she no longer had any hope. Clearly she had worn the device as a means of protecting herself from the pangs of death.

Plundering graves for bits of dead body, however ghoulish, is not incredible. Graves might be disturbed for a variety of reasons, of course: animals, especially carnivores, dug up dead bodies; flooding and erosion uncovered them; the widespread belief in vampires could and did lead to a corpse's being exhumed so that it could be checked and if necessary killed again, a practice which can be found well into the nineteenth century. So when we find that certain Scottish witches were accused of opening graves both within a kirk and within the kirkyard to pick out finger- and toe-joints and noses from which to make magical powders, we should bear in mind that the incident would not have seemed as extraordinary to its sixteenth-century audience as it does to us – although perhaps we should not be so surprised, since magical practices from beyond Western Europe (South African *muti*, for example), are known to use human parts in some of their medicinal unguents. So it is worth emphasising once again that medieval or early modern statements about witches and witchcraft need to be interpreted in the light of their contemporary social, cultural and religious background, and not of ours.

It is also worth noting that De Lancre, shocked as he was by the scale of the witchcraft he found in Labourd, as is evidenced by the huge number of children he says took refuge in the churches, seems to accept that even here witches can be rescued from the Devil and redeemed, since he refers to the 'nombre infiny des sorcieres gueries et remediees'. It is these people, along with other witnesses, who provide dramatic and (since they have been cured) reliable testimony to what the Labourdin witches had been doing until De Lancre and his fellow-commissioner Jean d'Espagnet arrived. This is somewhat unusual. Normally witnesses comprised people who had been affected by the witch's hostile magic; or confessing witches (repentant or not) who gave details of their personal activities and named others as their companions or accomplices when asked to do so; or unwitchers, men and women who were magical practitioners but not necessarily designated 'witches' themselves, and were sought out by people afraid they, or someone close to them, or some of their property such as a farm animal, had been bewitched, and wanted to know the name of the person responsible. Moreover, granting that witches could be cured was also to grant that being a witch might almost be regarded as something akin to being ill, as though the witch were a patient and her or his acts of witchcraft the symptoms of the disease from which she or he suffered. *Gueries* and *remediees* are essentially medical terms; yet De Lancre was not a physician. He was a lawyer who had no doubts that in Labourd he was witnessing the dreadful and frightening results of a whole people's being taken over by Satan in a kind of mass demonic possession.

Pierre de Lancre (1553–1631) was born in Bordeaux where his father was a *conseiller-notaire* and a royal secretary. After secondary education with the Jesuits, De Lancre went on to study law at Turin, gaining his doctorate in 1579, and then to protracted travels which took him round Italy and Bohemia – an indulgence which perhaps only someone from a fairly well-to-do family could have afforded – before returning to Bordeaux where in August 1583 he became a *conseiller au parlement*, and in 1588 married Jehanne de Mons, the grandniece of Montaigne. In 1600, a Jubilee year, he went on pilgrimage to various holy places including the Holy House of Loretto, and while in Naples met a young girl who, it was claimed, had been changed for a while by the Devil into a fat boy. Perhaps this encounter with the fluid boundaries between internal states and external appearances, which magic not only encouraged but also manipulated, set him thinking about what he referred to as 'inconstance' in the title of two of his books, *Tableau de l'inconstance des mauvais anges et démons* (1613), which is the one we shall be discussing in this chapter, and *Tableau de l'inconstance et instabilité des choses* (1607), a moralising work intended to illustrate the impermanence of the world in which the Devil is allowed to operate.

Le livre des princes (1617) represents a break from his preoccupation with the preternatural forces of evil and offers political advice to rulers, but he found himself unable to stay away from his main interests for very long, and *L'incredulité et mescréance du sortilège plainement convaincue* (1622), produced twelve years after his long personal engagement with witches and witchcraft, spends an impressive amount of learning upon showing that magic of any kind is not an illusion and should not be dismissed by those who are pleased to think otherwise. This work aroused the ire of Gabriel Naudé, at one time physician to Louis XIII and later librarian to Cardinal Barberini, who in 1625 published a fierce response, *Apologie pour tous les grands personnages qui ont esté faussement soupçonnés de magie*, to which De Lancre, duly irritated, replied two years later with his final work, *Du sortilège*.

It was when he was fifty-five, however, that he was given the task which would bring him into prolonged contact with diabolic activity on a grand scale. In December 1608 Henri IV was informed about a dire situation in the Pays de Labourd, the extent of which is outlined in the commission he issued to De Lancre on 17 January the following year:

> Dearly and well-beloved, the gentry and inhabitants of our country of Labourd have informed us and have complained to us that for the past four years there has been found in this said country such a large number of male and female witches [*sorciers et sorcières*] that every place in it is, as it were, infected: whereby they are subjected to such suffering that they will be forced to abandon their houses and the country unless they are speedily afforded means to preserve themselves from constant acts of harmful magic of this kind.

Together with fellow-commissioner Jean d'Espagnet, who was President of the Parlement of Bordeaux and a writer of works on Hermetic magic, De Lancre set out in accordance with the King's instructions, conscious that he had what amounted to a free hand in dealing with a problem which seemed to have passed well beyond local control. They went into a territory which was, in many ways, as unfamiliar to them as the New World or Japan, and De Lancre's description of it and its culture bears resemblance to travellers' and missionaries' reports from those far-away countries. Labourd is situated in the extreme south-west corner of France and, in addition to its French component, borders upon both Spain and Navarre, with a long coastline in the west and mountainous regions to the east. Its geography is therefore as varied as its culture. The people spoke Basque along with French and Spanish, and maintained a difference in dress, hairstyle, and social and religious customs which set them quite apart from the rest of France – hence De Lancre's fascination and eagerness to record, almost as though he were an ethnographer as well as a lawyer. 'There are three thousand souls in this country of Labourd', he added, 'counting those who go to sea; and among this entire population there are few families which are not involved in witchcraft in some way'. One reason for there being so many, he says, was that missionaries in the Indies, Japan and elsewhere had been so successful in converting the natives to Christianity that the demons who had once inhabited those countries were now fleeing and taking up residence in Labourd. Scottish and English merchants making for Bordeaux had seen them coming through France – 'great flocks of demons in the form of frightening men'. 'Consequently, the number of witches in this country of Labourd is so large and there are so many delinquent souls to be found, that it is quite impossible to imagine one can rescue or uproot them by judicial methods' (*Tableau* Book 1, discourse 2, section 9).

Invasion by displaced demons was perhaps one explanation for the plethora De Lancre found during the months he spent investigating Labourd; but it was not the only one he recorded. The men, he said, were absent for long periods of time. They did not appear to love their country, their wives or their children; their lands and fields were left for the most part uncultivated; and when the men returned in winter, they spent their time eating and drinking. The habit of telling lies was endemic and thus (De Lancre observed) the people's laziness and deceit provided two ideal conditions in which Satan could recruit his devotees. Satan finds work for idle hands indeed, and when for so much of the year the country was peopled by women, children and old men – none of whom have any judgement or knows how to behave – Satan could manipulate them entirely as he pleased. Hence, the women became witches and the men turned into savages.

This attitude towards the people among whom he was obliged to live for much of 1609, while he endeavoured to find out what had caused a massive outbreak of witchcraft and diabolism in the region and struggled to restore order where there was clearly chaos, goes some way to explaining why De Lancre recorded in very great detail the most extraordinary and the most Gothic elements about the Sabbat, the Devil himself, witches' ointments, the mark, transvection through the air, and all the other trappings of witchcraft expressed through worship of Satan, which have left him with the reputation of being a gullible bigot who allowed himself to treat as genuine the heated fantasies of old people and young children. Now, the *Tableau* is a very long work, intended to give not only a comprehensive account of his time in Labourd but also a thoroughly detailed picture of the inhabitants. They were, after all, different from the French readership at whom his book was principally aimed in two significant ways. First, they were as exotic in their manner of life, customs and language as any Amerindians or Japanese, and so what they had to say about their personal experiences of witchcraft was enthralling as much for its differences from as for its similarities to the experiences of what De Lancre and the King would have seen as the more civilised French. Indeed, De Lancre's book is perhaps better compared with such travellers' accounts as Jean de Léry's *Histoire de Brésil* (1578), Urbain Chauveton's *Brief discours et histoire d'un voyage de quelques François en la Floride* (1579), or the various narratives of the Americas by Théodore de Bry, published between 1590 and 1602, rather than such learned treatises as Martín Del Rio's *Disquisitiones Magicae*. In fact, De Lancre himself constantly makes these comparisons. 'The Indians on the island of Hispaniola inhale the smoke of a certain herb called *cohoba*, become agitated, put their hands on their knees and rest their heads on top of them, and so remain for some time in ecstasy: after which they stand up, completely lost and confused, and recount extraordinary things about their false gods (whom they call *Cemis*). This is just what our female witches [*sorcières*] do when they come back from the Sabbat' (*Tableau* Book 1, discourse 2, section 8).

Secondly, it was unusual for an extensive region to be overrun by witches in the manner of De Lancre's Labourd. As we read his account of the numbers involved, especially children – at one of the four great yearly festivals, several (female) informants told him, 'they had seen more than twelve thousand, and Marguerite who was a seventeen-year-old girl from Saint-Pé told us, with some exaggeration, that there were as many people there as stars in the sky' (*Tableau* Book 2, discourse 1, section 5) – we are reminded of the proliferation of vampires which will transform everyone into the undead unless they can be checked by drastic methods. De Lancre's readers were therefore being given a detailed account of what an area looked and sounded like if Satan was allowed his own way; and the conclusions he offered the King in what was, after all, the official report of a Royal Commission, were both simple and brutal: France is too lenient. 'In France we put to death those who confess (along with the proofs and *indicia* required by our laws and ordinances), but not those who do not confess, in spite of there being proof against them... In Spain and elsewhere, they are executed... if there is proof they have been to the Sabbat, made a pact with the Devil, renounced God, the Blessed Virgin, and so forth, committed idolatry, worshipped Satan, and done everything else the other witches have usually done, without being charged with a single act of hostile magic... Consequently, all these considerations really do urge us to throw out our scepticism, turn aside from the gentle sentences given by our forebears, and bring royal councils and all good judges to make this general resolution in France and elsewhere – to punish with death those male and female witches (*sorciers*) who have done no more than go to several Sabbats, even though they have not been convicted of a single act of hostile magic' (*Tableau* Book 6, discourse 5, section 19).

So what had De Lancre been told to render him so harsh? A thousand and one details: but his lengthy description of the Labourdin Sabbats may serve as one – admittedly the most lurid – example. He begins Book 2, the whole of which he devotes to a discussion of the Sabbat, with the days and times chosen by the Devil to hold these meetings. 'The Devil, wishing to have everyone's first vows and acknowledgements, has also chosen the first day of the week, thereby believing he can have some advantage and in some way defy Christians and good souls'. Monday, then, was his initial choice, although more recently he had varied the day. People went to the Sabbat at midnight or midday, and they went in large groups from parish to parish because Satan liked to mock religious processions which did the same thing. These groups usually made for some deserted place far from habitation, where there was no danger of running into people one knew or passing travellers. 'The popular name [for such a place] is *aquelarre heath* which means "goat's heath", that is to say, the heath or moorland where the Goat holds his assemblies', a point which more than fifty witnesses attested. But Satan might prefer to hold his Sabbat at crossroads instead, a piece of information which came from Isaac de Queyran, who said he had been to a Sabbat held at the crossroads of Palais Galienne, not far from Bordeaux.

One point puzzled De Lancre. Was it actually Satan in his own person who presided over each one of the thousands of Sabbats taking place all over the world? Not necessarily, he concluded, since 'he can provide for each place a demon who will look like him in every respect'; and so the deception inseparable from the Devil began with his very appearance. This appearance, according to thirteen-year-old Marie d'Aguerre and several others, took the form of a goat, although there were those who averred he looked like 'a large dark tree-trunk without arms or feet, seated in a chair, with something like a big, frightening man's face'. Even when he did resemble a goat, however, there were notable differences from the genuine animal. Some witnesses said he had four horns, two at the front of his head and two behind; others (the larger number) that he had three, with some kind of light issuing from the one in the middle to provide illumination for the company and to light the candles of those female witches assisting at a parody of the Mass. Other witnesses described the demon as a tall man dressed in dark clothes, who did not want to be seen clearly and was ablaze from head to toe, with a face as red as iron coming out of the furnace. Sixteen-year-old Jeanette d'Abadie, however, described him as having one face in front of his head and one behind (like the Roman god Janus), while De Lancre says he was present at a trial during which Satan was said to be like a big black greyhound, or something like a large bronze bull lying on the ground. 'All these shapes', he observes, 'testify that he appears in various forms and takes the shape of several animals so that he will not be recognised, and that he accommodates himself to the intelligence of those he renders submissive to him, and who want to worship him'.

Here we are given a reminder (not the first), of one of the principal themes of De Lancre's *Tableau*, the changeability of demons, their fickleness, the state of flux in which they exist and which they generate. De Lancre had examined this topic before in another huge work, *Tableau de l'inconstance et instabilité des choses*, to which the *Tableau de l'inconstance des mauvais anges et démons* acts as a companion; for they both discuss and illustrate the overriding, overwhelming theme of how the Devil subverts the order of creation and reduces everything to confusion. De Lancre therefore saw his commission to assist in bringing back Labourd to some kind of morally regulated existence as a profoundly religious enterprise, as well as a political directive. In this he is at one with a demonologist such as Del Rio whose account of the depredations of witches may be couched in rather more general terms – although it should be noted that in the *Tableau* De Lancre spends a lot of time discussing other preternatural phenomena such as lycanthropy and divination – but whose sensibilities were equally shocked at the sight of the chaos engendered by a diabolically inspired combination of heresy and witchcraft.

The atmosphere of nightmare and fantasy created by De Lancre's lengthy account of the Sabbat is best seen in the famous engraving done especially for the 1613 second edition by the Polish artist Jan Ziarnko. Ziarnko specialised in crowd scenes, and his picture not only summarises the principal points made or alluded to in the *Tableau* but communicates, by its carefully staged composition, a sense of otherness and distortion whereby recognisable activities such as playing music and dancing, riding, cooking and eating shimmer away from reality as they enter a perspective in which the preternatural mingles on equal terms with the human and natural.

Dominating the centre and foreground of the picture are three plumes of smoke or steam rising from a cauldron whose fire is provided by burning skulls and bones. One female witch increases the heat with her bellows, while a salamander (the elemental spirit of fire), and a toad vomiting poison upon the flames, look on. Two other female witches, one holding snakes in her right hand, prepare to kill a toad they are holding between them by slicing it with the half-moon shape of a sickle. These emphases on poison allude to *veneficium*, an act of specifically poisonous magic, which the women are in the process of preparing: and to the left we see one major source of the physical poison, toads in a pool which is attended by children – four boys and perhaps one girl – armed with sticks. One boy is raising his, as if in the act of getting ready to beat the water. That the basic meaning of *veneficium* can be taken literally, De Lancre leaves us in no doubt; for he tells us that, 'there are two types of poison, one thick like ointment, the other liquid. [The witches] use the thick one to bewitch people, either by causing them to swallow it or by smearing it on their clothes...The liquid one they put in a small earthenware vessel with several holes in the bottom, like a watering-can, and through these they sprinkle as much of this lubricant as they can on the crops'. The effect is to raise a black cloud which ruins everything. 'They also make use of another poison of greenish water, although they cannot say of what it is composed. They rub it on their hands and then if they touch someone's clothing, that person dies, or is bewitched and wretched for the rest of his or her life'.

At the bottom right of the picture a group of five witches, all female, and five male demons, four of whom are winged in the manner of insects, sit round a table, eating from a central dish on which the remains of a child are visible. A toad watches them eat, while a cat turns its back on the group and nibbles on some kind of scrap. De Lancre was told by sixteen-year-old Jeannette d'Abadie this kind of thing really did happen. 'She saw tables groaning with victuals, but when you wanted to take any of them, you found nothing under your hand unless you had brought baptised or unbaptised infants thither. She had very often seen each of these served and eaten'. Between the table and the cauldron a shrieking woman peers out from the dark entrance to a hole in a hillside, or the entrance to a cavern. Her withered, pendulous breasts suggest she is old, and she is naked apart from a cloak or blanket which the wind appears to be blowing across her stomach.

Within the borders formed by the clouds steaming out of the cauldron, we see representations of the witches' transvection to the Sabbat. One witch rides on a goat with two children bouncing behind her; all three are naked; the woman has her mouth open, whether calling out or merely gaping at the speed of her journey is not clear. Others appear to be falling, as it were, down a river of air, three astride broomsticks, although we see only the naked backside of one, as her upper body is hidden by the smoke or steam. A fourth travels upon a hybrid monster. She is naked and carries snakes in her outstretched right hand, while her left clutches the ear of her animal-demon. A fifth woman rests provocatively upon a billow of the steam or smoke, her head and shoulders thrown back in the attitude of someone waiting for her lover. Flying demons in half-human, monstrous or insect shape accompany them, one small specimen perching itself on the end of the bare-buttocked witch's broom. Bones stripped of flesh and an arm severed at the elbow tumble down with them, a reminder that witches were accused of eating the dead and using parts of them for magical purposes.

To the spectator's left, three scenes of social intercourse and revelry attract our attention. At the top, a group of five women, fully clothed, is playing music – Catherine de Moleres, aged nineteen, saw people dancing to the sound of violins, trumpets or side-drums which, she said, 'produced a very loud harmony'. Below them, six naked women dance hand-in-hand in a circle, but back-to-back, because many if not most of the events which took place at a Sabbat were the reverse of what was acceptable or normal in ordinary society. Below them again, one sees a dense crowd of men and women, many elegantly dressed, with horned demons in the background. To the spectator's right we see two parallel scenes. A fully-dressed man talks animatedly to a naked woman with an attendant demon, while above there is a scene of dancing round a tree. Four women, three naked and one clothed, all facing inwards, are hand-in-hand with naked winged demons who are facing outwards. Finally, dominating the top right is Satan himself in the shape of a four-horned goat with a flaming torch rising between the horns. He is seated on an elaborate throne which is flanked on each side by another. To his right sits a woman wearing a crown and carrying snakes in her right hand; to his left sits a nun, holding snakes in her left hand. The nun's throne also has toads perched on each of the two supporting pillars at her back. Thus, State and Church, both unnaturally represented by females, attend upon the Devil and look complaisantly upon a naked woman and a winged demon presenting a naked child, representative of innocence subverted and the future generation, to Satan either as servant or food or magic material.

Many of these features also appear in the accounts of Basque Sabbats reported to Alonso de Salazar Frías who was investigating a mass outbreak of witchcraft on the Spanish side of the border at the same time as De Lancre was grappling with the Labourdin problem. There was a queen of the *aquelarre*, a human witch, not a spirit; music was played by a band of witches; human flesh was served at a feast; and poisonous unguents and waters were manufactured there. Both Spanish and Labourdin Sabbats saw the celebration of a parody of the Mass, too, although Ziarnko chose not to illustrate this. It may have been too shocking for the public, although one should note that De Lancre had no hesitation in reporting the ceremony in detail, but perhaps Ziarnko just thought a depiction of it would not fit into the scheme he had devised for his engraving, a scheme which is, of course, symbolic and not narrative. Not only the dividing smoke or steam, but also the depiction of a rocky, largely barren landscape is devised in such a way that each group of figures actually forms a compact, self-

referential scene while, by having the legs or heads of individual participants intruding upon scenes above them and below, Ziarnko suggests that together they amount to a single impression of diabolism in
action.

But who were De Lancre's informants? The ones he quotes were
mainly young girls and women, although among his witnesses relating
to transvection and the Sabbat we find two boys aged ten and twelve,
one youth aged twenty-five, and one old man aged fifty-six.
Otherwise he is recording information from Catherine des Naguille
(eleven), Marie d'Aguerre (thirteen), Jeanne de Hortilopits and Marie
de Gastagualde (fourteen), Catherine d'Arreiouäque (fourteen or fifteen), Marie de Mariagrane (fifteen), Cristoual de la Garralde (fifteen
or sixteen), Marie de Naguille and Jeannette d'Abadie (sixteen),
Marguerite 'daughter of Sare', whose age appears as sixteen or seventeen, and as seventeen or eighteen, Marie Dindarte (seventeen), and
Marie d'Aspilcuette (nineteen). Three more women are aged twenty-
four, twenty-eight and thirty; one is more mature at forty; and then
came 'a witch from Villefranche' (forty-eight) and Catherine de
Barrende (about sixty). Overall, therefore, these ages tend to agree
with De Lancre's general observation that the men spent a long time
away at sea, leaving the land in the care of their women, their children
and their old people. Questioning principally teenagers about witchcraft in Labourd was thus not necessarily a deliberate choice on De
Lancre's part. Their evidence seems to have been largely all that was
available to him.

How did these witnesses come by their information? Mainly, they
said, from being taken to Sabbats from a very early age and there being
dedicated to Satan who, because their fathers were away from home so
much, became a kind of surrogate father to them, even down to the
child abuse which was common at the time, to judge by the frequency
with which incest appears in the records of criminal trials. Personal
experience, then, made them ideal testifiers against others whom they
claimed to have seen at such gatherings. But being an eye-witness was
not the only way of recognising who was a witch and who was not.
The mark left on a witch's body by Satan was, at the very least, a strong

indication. Indeed, De Lancre says firmly that such a mark is sure proof that the individual carrying it has been to a Sabbat. 'Several male and female witches [*sorciers*] confess as much when they are on the point of being thrown into the fire, when to deny it does them no good' (*Tableau* Book 2, discourse 2, section 13). The mark, however, did not necessarily appear only on the legs or arms or in the private parts. 'One girl, who claimed she could recognise male and female witches [*sorciers et sorcières*] from the first glance she gave them, told us that those from Biarrix had a mark like a toad's foot in their left eye, something which confessing witches from the same parish confirmed'. But De Lancre did not find this very helpful. 'We did not know how to verify this point, because neither this girl nor any other was able to explain succinctly how *we* could see these marks in that place, since she was convinced that a thorough-going witch sees, discovers and recognises things which only witches can see, and which those who have not taken "the toad's oath" cannot see' (*Tableau* Book 3, discourse 2, section 3).

At this point it is time – probably high time – for us to ask whether De Lancre believed what he and D'Espagnet were being told. The answer is usually taken to be a simple 'Yes', but I think that affirmative needs to be elucidated by being put in context. It is worth bearing in mind De Lancre's fascinated horror at the situation in a region he found at once exotic and reprehensible; a region whose way of life was so different from the order and civilisation to which he had been accustomed all his life; and, with only relative differences he had noticed in Italy, a region in which it appeared (to men ignorant of the culture and prejudiced against it) that almost anything, no matter how bizarre, might happen. There are several other aspects to De Lancre's mission we need to bear in mind.

First, De Lancre did not speak or understand the Basque language and therefore relied upon his interpreters; and his principal interpreter, as it happened, was a young priest, Lorenzo de Hualde, who had grown up in Labourd and was not only eager to co-operate with these French plenipotentiaries in the hope that his efforts would further his career, but was also a staunch believer in the reality of witches and every aspect of witchcraft, including the diabolic Sabbat. De Lancre was well aware of the difficulties inherent in his dependence on such an assistant. 'Right at the beginning of our commission, there appeared some small doubts which Satan engendered to favour the witches [*sorciers*] and hinder the execution of our purposes. A secular priest who had a good understanding of the Basque language offered to be our interpreter and explain witnesses' depositions and what the witches were saying at their hearings'. But De Lancre had reservations about accepting the priest's services, for 'even though he had a remarkable understanding of that language, nevertheless he could not convey its meaning to us in French with the same intelligence and exactitude, since Basque has such a forceful and specialised way of expressing itself that someone very competent and well-versed in French would be hindered from rendering the precise meaning of the Basque, something which was of the first importance and absolutely essential when it came to the confessions of witches [*sorciers*] and the hearing of witnesses' (*Tableau* Book 6, discourse 1, sections 1–2).

Indeed, De Lancre had a specific view on the task and quality of an interpreter. 'One must conclude', he said, 'that interpreters or mediums [should] not take it upon themselves to deviate from and should add nothing of their own to the cross-examinations which the judges ask them to undertake or to the criminals' replies... Interpreters are [to be] true echoes who remain absolutely silent if one does not speak... and do not make the slightest change in the words one says to them, pronouncing them in the same tone and with the same harshness one has used in speaking to them' (*Tableau* Book 5, discourse 1, section 6). Doubts therefore troubled him; but his adherence to the notion that witchcraft was a genuine phenomenon, and that since every accused, no matter where, was confessing more or less to the same things, hallucination or conspiracy were not credible as explanations of what they were saying, pressed him to accept the general truth of what he heard, even if he was not altogether happy with the way the information came to him. 'I have decided', he wrote in his preface to the whole work, 'to content myself with the simple recitation of the witnesses' depositions and the confessions of the accused, which have in them so much of what is unfamiliar that they will not fail to content the reader, even though I am leaving them in their unsophisticated and credulous form'. A straightforward and full record placed before the King and other readers would be sufficient to convince them of the reality of its contents, since the witnesses and witches were reporting, naïvely, ingenuously, but in the end convincingly, because they were confessing and recounting essentially the same experience.

Secondly, De Lancre had a political mission. The King wanted order restored, for if the Satanic chaos of Labourd were allowed to go unchecked, it might spread to the rest of France, an unthinkable prospect. While he was in Labourd, De Lancre stayed with the Comte d'Urtubie who was one of the important local secular authorities actively promoting and encouraging his commission against the Labourdin witches. Interestingly enough, the Comte was Lorenzo de Hualde's patron, and so we catch a glimpse of one of the local webs of friendship and obligation which almost always form part of the background to any prosecution of witches. Moreover, the Comte possessed estates in the Spanish Pyrenees and had a personal interest in those processes against witches, which were taking place in two villages in Navarre – Zugarramurdi and Vera-de-Bidasoa – at the same time. So not only did De Lancre have a pre-disposition to believe in the truth of witnesses and the witches' confessions, he was staying with someone purposefully engaged in their prosecution, and using the services of at least one priest whose personal interests were involved in making sure the information De Lancre received was couched to the detriment of those under suspicion. (To be fair to De Hualde, however, one should bear in mind that his personal ambition does not necessarily imply he was lying. It is perfectly possible for a person's belief and self-interest to coincide quite genuinely.)

But De Lancre may also have brought with him a very good reason to influence the Comte to co-operate in his mission. The full title of the *Tableau* expresses it succinctly: *A Picture of the Instability of Wicked Angels and Demons: wherein male and female witches* [sorciers] *and witchcraft receive full treatment. A book very useful to and necessary for not only judges but all those who live under Christian laws; with a discourse containing the procedure followed by the Inquisitors of Spain and Navarre in the case of 55 magicians, apostates, Jews and witches [sorciers] in the town of Logrigne in Castile, 9 November 1610; in which one sees how the exercise of justice in France is handled more in accordance with legal form and with more excellent conventions than in any other empire, kingdom, republic or state.* The emphasis is not simply upon judicial process, but upon *French* judicial process. The rule of *French* law is going to be re-established and imposed upon the Labourdins, and De Lancre is for the time being the principal arm of that law. When he leaves, the Comte d'Urtubie will accede to that responsibility in a new situation which will have seen the French King extend his hand over Labourd and firmly grasp the region with a fresh regime under which religious deviants of all kinds will find no place to enjoy or spread their horrors. It was therefore in both men's political interests, first to uphold the accusations of witchcraft, and then to see them through, under French legal provision, to the end the King desired.

But what shocked De Lancre perhaps more than anything was evidence that the Church in Labourd appeared either to have a remarkably lax view of how witches should be treated and punished, or to have abandoned God altogether and joined its flock in the blasphemous worship of Satan. What is more, it seemed that the Church in Spain and Navarre had a limited notion of her responsibilities when it came to dealing with Labourdin suspects who fled across the border.

They estimate there are thirty thousand souls in this country of Labourd, counting those who are at sea, and that among all these people there are very few families who do not come into contact with witchcraft in one way or another. 'If the number of witches [*sorciers*] condemned to the fire is so large', one of them said to us one day, 'it will be odd if I do not have a share in the cinders'. This is why one very often sees a son accuse his father and mother, a brother his sister, a husband his wife, and sometimes the other way round. This family link is why several heads of family, officers, and other people of the better sort, finding themselves affected by it, prefer rather to suffer the disability which may exist in this abomination (which witches [*sorciers*] are always afraid of when it comes to their families), than to see so many executions by gibbet, flame and fire, of people who are so closely related to them. We never had any doubt about proof. The multiplicity and infinite number [of witches] horrified us. At our arrival streams of them fled by sea and land, and both Lower and Upper Navarre and the Spanish frontier filled up with them, hour after hour. They pretended they were going on pilgrimage to Monserrat and Saint James [of Compostela]. Some claimed they were going to Terra Nova and elsewhere, and they raised so much alarm in Navarre and Spain that the Inquisitors came to the frontier and wrote to us, would we be kind enough to send them the names, ages and other distinguishing marks of the fugitive witches [*sorciers*] so that they could send them back to us which, they said, they would be very happy to do. We replied that we would be even happier if they kept them and looked after them and prevented them from returning, since we were more anxious to get rid of them than to have them back.

(*Tableau* Book 1, discourse 2, section 9)

This gives an indication of how relentlessly De Lancre pursued his task. Indeed, so severe was he that the local Archbishop, Bernard d'Eschaux, felt obliged to write to the King and to the Parlement of Bordeaux in an effort to have De Lancre's commission suspended or revoked and De Lancre himself sent home. It was a curious echo of the relationship between Heinrich Institoris, author of the *Malleus Maleficarum*, and George Golser, Bishop of Brixen, who in 1485 complained about Institoris's methods of investigating witchcraft and succeeded in blocking his progress. Bernard d'Eschaux, however, seems to have concealed his hostility from De Lancre, since the latter recorded of him that he had always shown his willingness to have 'this human plague' exterminated and to have his flock 'purged of this abomination' – a sentiment expressed in the medical terminology common when both theologians and lawyers wrote about witches or heretics.

Obstruction was one thing; but De Lancre could scarcely credit the actual participation of priests in the Sabbat itself. They attended in large numbers, too – Jeanne Dibatton (twenty-nine) and Marie de la

Ralde (twenty-eight) saw 'many priests [their pastors], curés, vicars and confessors' – and Marie observed further that she had greater pleasure in going to the Sabbat than in going to Mass, although she would have been able to attend Mass there anyway, of course, because the principal function of the priests who joined in the Sabbat was to celebrate it, 'clad in red and white'. Other young females reported further that at the place of the Sabbat there was an altar and above it 'a little demon, the size of a twelve-year-old child, which looks pretty and keeps perfectly still while this abominable secret ceremony and piece of ridicule is going on. But once it is over, both he and the altar vanish' (*Tableau* Book 6, discourse 3, section 2). Information about such a Mass also came from the priests of various parishes – De Lancre names 'Martin Detcheguaray, one called Escola, [Pierre] Bocal, and five others who escaped us' – whose collected depositions indicated that there was no part of the ceremony of the Mass and none of its usual accompaniments, such as music and lighted candles and even a sermon, which did not have their counterpart at this blasphemous parody, down to the elevation of a Host which was black rather than white, not the customary round shape but triangular, and lacked the usual sacred symbol stamped on one side. A fourteen-year-old from Saint Jean-de-Luz added his own grotesque detail to this. 'Father Jean Souhardibels, in the place called "la Cohandia", made the elevation, showing a black Host, and was himself raised upside down in the air with his head hanging down in front of the Devil, and so remained throughout the elevation' (*Tableau* Book 6, discourse 3, section 9).

Can we believe any of this? Once again, it is important to qualify one's answer. Priests had undoubtedly been involved in magic since very early times and had not hesitated to make use of the Mass to consecrate amulets and other magical objects. Indeed, to judge from several manuscript grimoires of the Middle Ages and later, many altars must have been littered with all kinds of bits and pieces, hidden under the altar-cloth, while the priest carried out his grimoire's instructions to say Mass over them so many times, or on such-and-such holy days. The Mass could also be perverted for other magical ends. Father Philibert Delmeau, for example, was arrested and put on trial in 1624 after confessing that, in order to help a newly married groom who was suffering from impotence caused by witchcraft, he had, at the prompting of his personal demon, said a Mass backwards, and by this means had undone the bewitchment. So, in the face of a great deal of external evidence that some clergy engaged in magical operations, even to the extent of abusing the Mass for such purposes, we should not be surprised to find that accusations of priests' involvement in the Sabbat were widespread, and that people found these assertions perfectly believable. The details provided by witnesses may often have been fantastic in themselves, and there is no reason to presume that De Lancre – or any other similar investigating official – found every one of them convincing. But neither he nor they had any difficulty with the basic proposition and, given some priests' known activities, one should hardly be surprised.

Three Labourdin priests were put on trial before the Parlement of Bordeaux in January 1611. One of them confessed everything and signed his confession three times. The other two offered no confession, but were condemned to death in spite of this because of the large number of witnesses who kept coming forward to testify against them. Arancete, Vicar of Handaye, had by contrast only nine or ten witnesses to his crimes, but these were sufficient to testify that he had attended the Sabbat a hundred times, renounced Christ, the Virgin and the saints, worshipped the Devil, said Mass at the Sabbat, and avowed publicly that he was going to defend witches against Jesus Christ (whom he contemptuously referred to as 'Jannicot'). Three other priests escaped into Spain and Navarre, but two more, Lasson and De Haritourena, who had fled into Spain and spent nine months on the run disguised as labourers, finally made the mistake of venturing back into France where they were captured and brought before the criminal court on 4 May 1610.

The emergence of such detailed and plentiful evidence against several priests was shocking and De Lancre forthrightly maintained that it was elements of corruption in the Church which made the further corruption of her priests, if not inevitable, at least easier. 'It is not possible that these priests who have vowed to serve God can serve two masters. All the simonies and secrets and other lawsuits and quarrels one finds among churchmen are more properly suited to this place [the Sabbat] than any other' (*Tableau* Book 6, discourse 4, section 3) – and, as if to underline his point, De Lancre goes on to use an extraordinary term to describe such a renegade: 'the priest who celebrates Mass at the Sabbat is the real *succubus* of the benefice which God has entrusted to him'. The *succubus* was a demon in female form who had sexual intercourse with men. To liken a priest to such a demon was, therefore, to point the finger not only at his corruption but also, since women were regarded as intellectually, morally and physically frail, to his non-manly weakness, the ultimate cause of his allowing himself to be seduced by Satan. So, if the Church herself could not be trusted to present an impregnable bulwark against the assaults of the Devil, who could? Priests should be guarding their flocks against the Enemy; but who, in the words of Juvenal, would guard the guards themselves? De Lancre's answer was quite straightforward. If the Church could not do the job, the state would have to take over this responsibility. Nor could the Church complain, for she already depended upon the state to safeguard her own temporal establishment. 'Even priests and other ecclesiastics, in order to save themselves and guarantee the jurisdiction of the Church, enjoy the great privilege of being able to run and put themselves under the protection of the temporal jurisdiction' (*Tableau* Book 6, discourse 4, section 9). Not surprisingly, therefore, De Lancre was happy to be able to report to the King that several of these individuals had been brought in front of the secular courts which then administered appropriate justice.

That De Lancre took a severe course against the witches he found in Labourd, both ecclesiastical and secular, cannot be contested. That he relied upon masses of unverified and, in some cases, unverifiable testimony is also true. That he was driven, at least in part, by political agenda from Paris, which sought to suppress Labourd and bring it much more firmly under French control, is clear enough. But was he, as Baroja called him, merely 'one of the most absurd figures of the movement to repress witchcraft'? It is very easy to write him off in this way, especially if one approaches him on purely twenty-first-century terms without making an effort to see and understand him on his own and in the context of his own period. It would take too long to offer a complete discussion here, but there is one telling comparison he makes, which is very illuminating,[3]

> I remember seeing in this country an automaton in the form of a fountain which was taken all round France. It demonstrated a kind of perpetual motion by taking some water from a vessel which acted as a reservoir and constantly returning it to the same place, as to its source. The water passed through several channels, making use of a universe of wheels and pumps, and created an infinite number of beautiful effects. This fountain exactly represents the Sabbat. It set in motion a circlet of people who danced round, two by two, always a man with a woman. Then a single woman came into view and was put on display, dancing all alone like a star of the show on the outside of the circle. After her came a grotesque who held a small basket under his arm, and when it opened the lid, out came a man's head which the grotesque struck two or three times with a club and made it go back inside the basket again. Then two or three other grotesques played so skilfully on the drum, with head-movements so deliberate and so pleasantly contrived that even their eyes rolled in their heads, to the great astonishment of the most inquisitive spectator. Then one heard certain bells, so tuned that they emitted a loud, melodious and pleasing sound.
>
> But all these wheels, all these movements, all these dances and jollities, were held in contempt when one saw that the cause of all this motion was an old dog shut up in a leather wheel which was ripped and scratched from his paws. One also saw that the water was stagnant and stinking and was of no use for anything except to make people wet and annoyed; and all these hoops, all these springs, all these wheels and movements, all these drums were only something hateful, an advertisement for the war. It was nothing but jesters and grotesques which really did make merry, dance and embrace, but which did so by artifice.
>
> (*Tableau* Book 6, discourse 2, section 5)

Just like the Sabbat? De Lancre was not comparing the two detail-for-detail, of course. What he meant was that when those he was interrogating told him they had been to a Sabbat and had seen a variety of things there, which they proceeded to describe in terms both vivid and specific, they were telling him the truth. Yes, they had been transvected as they said, and yes, they had indeed seen and done what they said they had seen and done. But in fact, in reality as God sees it, the whole thing was an illusion created by Satan working away in the background, like the automaton's prisoner-dog, to persuade his audience that what they were seeing was somehow to be trusted. So, to the alleged participants of the Sabbat, their experiences were real in the same way as a conjuring-trick is real; the elements which make up the trick are substantial enough, but the dénouement is, in spite of appearances, a fiction intended to deceive. Thus De Lancre makes a profound comment on the relationship between the preternatural and the natural worlds, and lets us see that relationship simultaneously with both divine and human eyes; and he also tacitly explains why he, and so many others of his contemporaries, were willing and able to accept as true what we, forgetting to look with the two-fold vision of the earlier period, find incredible and absurd.

3

BATTISTA CODRONCHI:
THE MEDICAL VIEWPOINT

Martín Del Rio was in no doubt that the cause of certain illnesses lay in witchcraft. 'With God's permission', he wrote, 'witches [*sagae*] afflict a fair number of living creatures with very serious illnesses or death by means of their acts of harmful magic'. Witchcraft, in fact, had profound effects upon the bodies of its victims who might contract fevers, suffer from fits, or become weaker and weaker until death supervened or the malefice was lifted. They might find themselves impotent, their milk might dry up, or they might be possessed by at least one evil spirit and thus exhibit the great range of symptoms (such as vomiting small and large objects, twisting their bodies into grotesque postures, or appearing to speak with someone else's voice), which were familiar through the descriptions of exorcists and physicians.

For all this, religion provided remedies: prayer, fasting, exorcism and, in the case of Catholics, the use of sacramentals such as holy water; and not all of these should necessarily be regarded as purely spiritual answers to the problem. Battista Codronchi, who is to be the focus of this chapter, maintained, for example, that because confession alleviated a patient's fear of mortal sin, it could be regarded as a physical medicament since body and soul were linked and liable to have effects one upon the other (*De Christiana ac tuta medendi ratione*,

47–48). But because the effects of witchcraft made themselves known through physical, morbid symptoms, medical treatments of one kind or another were also available, one type provided by university-trained physicians, the other by healers who, despite modern assumptions to the contrary, were by no means always a cheap alternative. In July 1654, for example, George Groat from Canisbay in Scotland was on his deathbed and his daughter Isobel Groat, leaving the house in some distress, met a woman known simply as 'Graycoat' who asked her if she was weeping for the dying man. Isobel answered that she was, where-upon Graycoat offered to cure him of his illness which, she said, had its origin in bewitchment. She was offered payment in the form of a cow or a horse, both rather expensive in a rural economy, but actually refused, saying she would cure him by taking a life for a life: in other words, she would transfer his illness into someone else (or perhaps an animal), who would then die in his place, an offer George's wife refused when she was told, preferring to leave his fate in the hands of God. In this rejection, however, she was somewhat unusual. Most peo-ple paid the price and accepted the consequence.

'Cunning folk', 'magare', 'curanderas' and 'guérisseurs', as non-qual-ified medical practitioners might be known, frequently specialised in treating a single ailment and in diagnosing whether an illness had a natural or preternatural cause. But, specialist or not, they usually employed techniques which involved herbal concoctions for internal or external use, prayers or verbal formulae which might be spoken aloud intelligibly or muttered almost in secret, and ritual gestures such as making the sign of the cross. Variations could make their treatments more elaborate, of course, but we may note at once that the employ-ment of words and gestures, even though these could be entirely Christian in origin or intent, might be sufficient in themselves to raise questions in the minds of state or ecclesiastical officials. If the remedies were Christian, why would the patient choose to consult a cunning person rather than a priest, who not only had the power to make these words and gestures effective, but was legally permitted to use them? Or, in the case of Protestant doubters, were not these words and ges-tures reminiscent of Catholic practice and tradition, in which case were they not condemnable as both superfluous and superstitious? By whose power were the cunning person's operations intended to work? If the illness she or he was treating were natural, what need for words and gestures? If it had been caused by witchcraft, could not the cunning person's actions be interpreted as counter-magic, itself impermissible as an answer to any preternatural problem?

In fact, two things more than anything else separate cunning remedies from university medicine. First, there are the supernatural or preternatural assumptions underlying the outlook of both the cunning person and her or his clients. Even if they diagnosed the illness as natural, they were unlikely to use natural remedies unsupported by words and gestures a university-trained doctor would be inclined to view as unnecessary, even if the patient were comforted and thus eased by their employment. Secondly, the doctor was not believed to have caused the disease (although his treatments might kill his patient), whereas there was always the possibility that the cunning person or witch brought in to effect a cure had laid the illness on to start with. Indeed, it was not uncommon for a suspect witch to be fetched forcibly to someone's bedside to undo what the patient and her family were convinced she had caused. In October 1654, for example, George Turner's wife Isobel, after spending some time chatting to Margaret Erskine, was saying goodbye to her at the door when she suddenly fell down in what appeared to be a dead faint. Margaret had been gathering a reputation as a witch, so when George came home and found his wife lying unable to move and in great pain, he put her to bed and then took an axe and went to look for Margaret, threatening her and blaming her for his wife's condition. 'Whereupon', says the record, 'the said Margaret came into the house with him and laid her hand upon [Isobel's] head and said, "I hope you will be well"; and immediately she recovered her perfect heart and senses as formerly'.

People did discriminate, of course. Not every illness was thought to be caused by witchcraft, although telling the difference might not be easy. 'Diseases caused by malefice', wrote Codronchi, 'are very difficult to recognise, so much so that physicians have their doubts', and his views were echoed by the German physician Daniel Sennert

(1572–1637) who proffered three signs whereby a venefic illness might be recognised:

> First and foremost is this sign of illnesses caused by workers of poison-ous magic: that even the most learned physicians have their doubts in recognising the illness. They hesitate, are completely undecided, and can scarcely come to a firm conclusion which will satisfy them; and although they use many remedies, these do no good at all and the ill-ness becomes worse day by day. Secondly, where natural illnesses begin gradually and take their time to arrive at their full-blown state, illnesses caused by the Devil often seem to establish themselves sud-denly in full vigour, often without any natural causes being present or disorder of the humours; and the patient suffers very severe pains and other symptoms. Thirdly, the patients exhibit unusual symptoms, and symptoms which their doctors have scarcely come across before. They are roasted by pain, first in one part of their body, then in another. Very many of them lose weight all over their body for no reason. They become melancholic and some of them suffer from various con-vulsions. Some people add further that if a witch [saga] or a worker of poisonous magic [veneficus] comes to visit the sick person, the patient immediately begins to feel worse and is seized by trembling and a feeling of horror. If the patient is a child, it cries and one sees some other physical change. If needles, knives, and similar man-made objects, or other which cannot be produced inside the human body are ejected either by vomiting or by some other means, or break out, or are pulled out of ulcers and abscesses, this is a very reliable sign of an illness caused by veneficium.
>
> (*Practica medicina* Book 6, part 9, chapter 6)

To these details, Codronchi adds that sufferers from preternatural ill-nesses frequently have laboured (also known as 'distressed') breathing for no obvious cause. Some people lose the will or desire to do anything; some vomit up their food, and in consequence their stom-ach becomes upset to the point where quite often they suffer pain because of their retching; and they may also notice a heavy weight in the belly, or something rising and falling up and down their gullet. Other symptoms include a pricking or stabbing pain in the area round the heart; the big veins in the neck can be seen to throb; there may be pain in the kidneys, or a very cold or a very hot wind suddenly entering and leaving the stomach. Some people are rendered impotent, suffer light sweats, especially at night, or feel as though small separate sections of the body have been tied up in knots, along with 'many other unusual symptoms and morbid conditions which are perhaps as yet unknown to medical science' (*De morbis veneficis* 3.13). It is interesting that the trained physician should reserve the right to re-classify certain afflictions should medical knowledge uncover their origins as natural rather than demonic, especially perhaps in Codronchi's case, since he was convinced that many illnesses did indeed have their causes in the actions of evil spirits often aided by human agency in the form of witches. But in fact he had not always been of this opinion, or at least not so strongly attached to it, as his early writings suggest.

Born on 27 August 1547 in Imola, he attended school there before going to read medicine at the University of Bologna. Returning to Imola to practise, he tried to embark on a political career but was forced by his own poor health to surrender the notion and concentrate on medicine. His first published book (1597) was a medico-therapeutic study of the mineral waters of the hot springs at Riolo and Valsenio, both only a few miles south of Imola, the former known and exploited since ancient times; but his real interest was in forensic medicine and medical ethics, and in 1589 he published 'Cases of Conscience relating primarily to Physicians', followed in 1591 by a work which made him famous, *De Christiana ac tuta medendi ratione* (The Safe, Christian Way of Curing People). Beginning with an unacknowledged quotation from Erasmus – 'theologians take a person's character as their starting-point, whereas physicians begin with the body' – Codronchi argues, with copious illustrations drawn from the Church Fathers, that a doctor's behaviour and relationship with his patient should, even in the smallest details, be governed by Christian principles. Thus, a patient who disobeys her or his doctor commits a sin because the doctor is exercising a legitimate authority (*De*

Christiana ratione, 139–43). On the other hand, a doctor's fee should be regulated according to how much he has had to do to help the patient and how much the patient can afford to pay (*Ibid.*, 89).

Notable to modern eyes is his prohibition (Book 1, chapter 37) against a patient's consulting Jewish doctors or a Christian doctor's collaborating with them, 'unless necessity compels him to summon them, as when, for example, no Christian doctors are available, or when the Christian doctors are not able or are not in a position to cure the patient's illness'. This looks like straightforward anti-Semitism, and there may indeed be something of that in his remarks, especially those which repeat the standard cliché of the day that Jews were taught a variety of tricks intended to harm Christians rather than help them. But one also needs to bear in mind two modifying points. First, the whole intention of Codronchi's book, as shown by the title, is to argue that the practice of medicine ought to take place in conjunction and harmony with *Christian* theology; and secondly, there was a long tradition which associated Jews with magic, and in consequence Codronchi may have had the uneasy feeling that the prescriptions of Jewish doctors might be a touch too close to the magic of what could be seen in cunning or 'popular' remedies for the comfort of his own or his colleagues' consciences.

Four years later, in 1595, he published a treatise on forensic medicine, *Methodus testificandi*, and the work which makes him relevant to this discussion, *De morbis veneficis ac veneficiis* (Illnesses caused by Poisons and Acts of Poisonous Magic). His motive in writing something so different from his usual topics of interest lay, as he tells us, in a personal incident:

A number of years ago, my daughter Francesca, who was ten months old and in the care of a wet-nurse, was afflicted by an extraordinary loss of weight, and with ever-increasing frequency her breath would come in loud gasps. When her swaddling-bands were taken off, she would always wail and cry and behave as though she were sick, quite unlike the way children act during the removal of the bandages, since they are usually quiet and take pleasure in the process even though they may be in discomfort or experiencing some distress or physical pain. We found no preternatural cause for her condition but we changed the wet-nurse. However, Francesca continued to decline and my wife began to suspect that because the child was rather pretty, she had aroused the envy or hatred of some elderly woman who had produced these harmful effects by means of poisonous magic [*veneficium*]. So my wife searched the mattress and found several signs of *veneficium*, namely, chick-peas, coriander-seeds, a scrap of charcoal and a fragment of bone taken from a corpse, and a lump of something I did not recognise, but which an experienced exorcist told me was the kind of thing made by these offensive, shameless women I have been discussing [i.e. witches] from various substances mixed with menstrual blood. In addition to this, there were some feathers skilfully sewn together so that they could easily be attached to a cap, as is the fashion.

We burned all these in a fire which had received a blessing. Exorcisms were carried out for three days and other holy remedies applied, and she began to recover and put on weight, to the extent that we thought she had been cured. Nevertheless, a few days later she was very disturbed and was beginning to cry a lot, so we searched her bed again and found several more bits of magical apparatus [*instrumenta*] which we burned. She seemed to be restored to health, but on the day of the full moon that month she spent the whole night sleepless and crying. Next morning her colour had turned ashen, and her physical appearance was so changed from what it had been the previous evening that it made us tearful and astonished in equal measure. Yet again we searched her bed and found two small pieces of dried nut and white bone, nine or ten fish-bones which had been fashioned into hair-combs, and some little garlands put together with remarkable skill from various objects. After these had been surrendered to the fire, we went to live in another house, and when an experienced exorcist had employed every other, more powerful remedy [at his disposal], by God's kindness she recovered without any natural remedy.

So perhaps God permitted the *veneficium* so that I might experience in my own daughter something to which I used to give too little credit when it happened to other people; and so that I might recognise and cure their illnesses, I began to look for books which would tell me about this kind of thing, to read them, and to believe what they said. I learned a great deal from them and from an experienced exorcist and from observing many patients; and I have willingly undertaken this work with the aim of bringing relief to others. Among the various authors I happened to read was Claudius Gulliaudus, a very learned exponent of Holy Scripture, who in his commentary on Saint Paul's *Epistle to the Galatians*, deals with bewitchment [*fascinum*] and describes my daughter's illness exactly. He says some people call it by its French name, *le mal de Vauldorzerie*, and that it makes small children waste away, lose weight, and twist themselves out of shape in a distressing fashion. Sometimes they scream and cry without stopping, all of which symptoms and signs I observed in my daughter; and everyone will be able to appreciate how true these things are, since this same illness, which is demonic in origin, together with these same signs, is being caused at the present time by *veneficia* in Romagna and in France, and has been so these many years past.

(*De morbis veneficis* 1.8)

As we can see from this catalogue of symptoms, it is not surprising that Codronchi and his wife became convinced that their daughter's illness – sometimes known as the *Waldensian*, that is, the witches' disease – had a magical origin. Dismissing the wet-nurse was an obvious and reasonable precaution against further bewitchment. It is not that people believed nurses were particularly prone to witchcraft, although the common medical notion that a wet-nurse's character might transmit itself to the child through her milk meant that the choice of wet-nurse was a consideration of very great moment and that no risks should be taken in case of the child's irregular health or behaviour. The Italian polymath Girolamo Cardano (1501–76) was quite explicit:

Choose a nurse who is not blind in one eye, given to drink, sick or morally depraved. A half-blind woman will make the child half-blind, not through her milk but because she is always looking at him. A drunk makes it likely he will get the shakes; she takes away his strength and will make him prone to drink and lack of self-control. Most of all, the nurse can shape his habits and his body – to such an extent that if her eyes are very dark, she will cause the child's eyes to become dark, even if they were very pale by nature.

(De subtilitate Book 11)

It is rather that babies and young children were thought to be especially vulnerable to envy and the malice or spite which might flow therefrom, and that in consequence anyone with an evil eye could look at a child and pass on harm or illness. This is why Signora Codronchi suspected *fascinatio* – the casting of evil through a glance – an ancient belief going back at least as far as the Greeks whose verb *baskainein* (later *phaskainein*) meant 'to grudge or envy' and passed into Latin as a word for an evil spell. The Greeks had theories about how the evil eye was supposed to work and transmit its innate maleficence. Plutarch, for example, explained that all bodies emit effluxes through the pulsating warmth which naturally accompanies life. The eyes in particular are easily set in motion thereby and emit a kind of power, and because they are susceptible to movement, they respond quickly to movement in other eyes. Thus, because the eyes are placed near the soul, an eye which looks at another conditioned by envy or spite will be affected by those emotions which stream from the ill-natured eye in the form of small images *(Moralia* 680 C–D).

Some of these notions depend on Democritus, others on pseudo-Aristotle's *Problemata*, and it was certainly the latter which guided later discussions of the subject, since the work was thought to be a genuine Aristotelian treatise. Martín Del Rio, meticulous as always in his treatment of any subject, says that there were three types of 'fascination':

(1) bewitchment by glance or facial expression,
(2) a kind of contagious disease similar to inflammation of the eyes or love, and
(3) a destructive quality originating with evil spirits.

All three, of course, could coalesce in practice and thus be indistin-
guishable from one another. Daniel Sennert tells us further that people
believed it was possible to harm a child not only intentionally but also
inadvertently by offering him or her a word or two of praise.
Therefore whenever anyone uttered a commendation, it was customary to add 'God keep you safe', meaning 'God grant this praise may
not harm you or cast an evil spell on you'; a belief, he says, which may
justly be considered superstitious and yet is not entirely without foundation, and whose remedies are not completely condemnable (*De
infantium curatione* Part 2, chapter 32). Hence the custom of decking a
child's neck with an amulet, very often in the shape of an erect penis,
to ward off the evil eye, a custom which is still followed in various
parts of the world, especially round the Mediterranean.

Signora Codronchi associated the evil eye with an unspecified
woman of mature years. Battista uses the words *vetula* to describe her, a
diminutive (so to speak) of *vetus* meaning 'old', and therefore an indication that the woman was older than 'young' but not as old as 'old'.
Early modern writers on witches, however, often referred to their subjects as old, and this has passed on into modern times to give the standard image of the witch. But the picture is very misleading and people
during the earlier period by no means looked in practice for the old
when they were searching out women suspected of malicious magic.
The tradition stems partly from Greek and Roman antiquity which
offered literary portraits of female magicians such as Circe or Medea,
who were young and beautiful, and Canidia who was old and ugly.

Illustrations of witches tend to include both these types. Popular
woodcuts such as one finds accompanying ballads and pamphlets are
often too crude to allow one to establish the age of the witches concerned except by reference to the text itself, and not always even then.
Perhaps the most frequently reproduced examples come from
Francesco Maria Guazzo's *Compendium Maleficarum* (1608), and these
simply show a mixture of men and women taking part in activities
connected with the Sabbat. The women are fashionably dressed and
give the impression of youth or maturity rather than old age; but there
is no accurate telling whether they are meant to be girls, women or

crones. Some painters deliberately chose the age of their subjects. Dosso Dossi's picture of Circe shows her as young, as one might expect, as do 'The Witchcraft of Love' attributed to Van Eyck, the 'Four Witches' and 'Two Witches' of Albrecht Dürer, and the 'Four Witches' of the eighteenth-century painter Léonard Defrance. On the other hand, Dürer (again) and Jacques de Gheyn have both given us pictures of old, shrivelled, hag-like witches, the former of a single figure, the latter of three witches looking for hidden treasure. But actually it seems to have been more common to portray witches in a group consisting of both young and old women, with the emphasis on the young, and Hans Baldung Grien, Hans Franck, David Teniers le jeune, Franz Francken le jeune, and Adrian Huybrechts, for example, all present such scenes depicting either the departure for the Sabbat or the Sabbat itself.

Literature, however, meaning both scholarly and popular works on witches, generally preferred to concentrate on the witch-as-hag, for which there may have been more than one reason. First, it is possible that many suspect witches were indeed old by the time they were arrested. In case after case we hear that the accused had been involved in incidents of suspected magic stretching back ten, twenty, thirty years, and whether one believes the accuracy of the details of each magical charge is of no relevance to the point that the accused had been gradually acquiring a reputation for practising witchcraft over a long period of time. If she was old when she was finally arrested, she had been young or mature when her neighbours' suspicions began. The perception of the witch as old may thus be true up to a point, but should not be taken as necessarily the whole truth.

Secondly, it was easier to dismiss old women as deluded and silly than it was to brush aside the young if one wanted to suggest that witchcraft, or at least many aspects of it, were illusory and so not to be feared. Thus the Englishman Reginald Scot argued that accused witches should be treated with some degree of leniency because,

> they which are commonlie accused of witchcraft, are the least suffi-
> cient of all others to speake for themselves; as having the most base

and simple education of all others; the extremitie of their age giving
them leave to dote, their povertie to beg, their wrongs to chide and
threaten (as being void of any other waie of revenge), their humor
melancholicall to be full of imaginations, from whence cheefely pro-
ceedeth the vanities of their confessions.

(*The Discoverie of Witchcraft*, epistle to his readers)

Senility, poverty, personal malice, possible dementia – all these may
well have been present in some who were apprehended as witches; but
we have plenty of evidence that many were neither old nor wandering
nor poor, and so we need to be careful not to seize upon passages such
as this because they appear to be consonant with and support modern
scepticism. The scepticism of the earlier period tended to relate not to
the existence of evil spirits and their ability to do harm to humans if
God permitted, but to the more extravagant claims made by many
witches, such as their flight through the air to a Sabbat or their power
to change their shape from human to animal. Thus the German physician Johann Wier (1515–88), often cited as a 'sceptic' in the modern
sense of the word, argues that because witches (*lamiae*) are melancholic, feeble-minded, depressed old women, the Devil is more easily
able to use them as his instruments, deceiving them into false confessions by filling their minds with illusions whereby the women imagine that they themselves have done harm to others *when in fact the harm
has been effected by the Devil or by one of his evil spirits* (*De praestigiis daemonum* Book 6, chapter 8, my italics).

Thirdly, the early modern period had the belief that everything in
nature had its antithesis and in consequence creation could be viewed
as an enormous complex of contrarieties. Hence Francisco Sánchez, a
mid-sixteenth-century Portuguese physician, wrote: 'All nature con-
sists of contraries and is preserved by contraries, as by matter, form and
privation; hot and cold; wet and dry; good and evil; generation and
corruption; life and death; happiness and sorrow; summer and winter;
north and south; good fortune and bad fortune; war and peace; riches
and poverty; fertility and sterility; virtue and vice; piety and impiety'
(*De divinatione per somnum*). We should therefore expect to find

witches depicted as both young and succulent, and as old and barren, partly representing contrariety within the category 'witch' itself, and partly mirroring the double tradition inherited from Classical antiquity, of which scholars and well-educated painters would have been aware.

Lastly, it is worth bearing in mind that the identification of the witch as old and stupid could serve confessional polemic rather well, as it could be made to suggest aged/silly/outdated/Catholic as opposed to young/modern/realistic/Protestant, a tactic of which English polemicists especially availed themselves. So we find the Archbishop of York, Samuel Harsnett, describing the 'typical' witch as 'an old weather-beaten croane, having her chinne and knees meeting for age, walking like a bow leaning on a shaft, hollow-eyed, untoothed, furrowed on her face, having her lips trembling with the palsie', a portrait which appears in his *Declaration of Egregious Popish Impostures* (1603), a blast against recent exorcisms performed by a Jesuit and other Catholic priests, which had caused a great stir in London; John Wagstaffe maintaining that witches' confessions were actually dictated to them 'by the very Inquisitors themselves, with a design to advance the reputation of the Virgin Mary, and the Sacraments of their own Church' (*The Question of Witchcraft Debated*, 1669); and Reginald Scot, a virulent anti-Catholic, writing to his cousin that 'infidelitie, Poperie, and manie other manifest heresies be backed and shouldered, and their professors animated and hartened, by yeelding to such creatures such infinit power as is wrested out of Gods hand, and attributed to witches' (*The Discoverie of Witchcraft*, epistle to Sir Thomas Scot).

Nevertheless, when all these points are taken into consideration, there remains the fact that Signora Codronchi associated the evil eye with an older rather than a younger woman, and for that she had (although it was unlikely she was aware of it) respectable medical support. It is perhaps most clearly expressed by Antonio de Cartagena, Professor of Medicine at the University of Alcalá between 1510 and 1532. In 1530 he published a treatise on the subject, *Libellus de fascinatione*, which is one of the earliest attempts to define the evil eye and its operation (*fascinatio*) in terms of a disease. 'It is possible', he wrote, 'that a person whose humours are corrupt emits vapours from his or her eyes and infects the air, and that the air affects children, who are not able to resist it very well because of their exceptional delicacy'; and he noted further that *fascinatio* was real 'because very many children are infected, and very many of those who have been subject to it die'.

The Latin verb here translated 'infect' also means 'impregnate (with some substance), taint, poison', and this range of meanings is very significant, for it helps to explain why women rather than men were thought to exercise the evil eye. It was a commonly accepted notion that women's bodies were more noxious than those of men. Menstruation – partly a curse inflicted on women after the Fall, partly a physical purgation of excess fluid – had a long history as a poisonous source both of women's inferiority to men and of their potentiality to exude a hostile magic. Both Aristotle and Pliny the Elder, for example, said that menstruating women emitted vapours from their over-heated menstrual blood, which escaped through their eyes and was capable of clouding or staining mirrors, a version of events which was repeated by Cartagena and many others. In young women, this blood is expelled, wrote Cartagena. 'In older women, however... because the paths by which it is expelled have become very narrow and their power to expel it is weak, it happens that they often have menstrual blood in their veins'. Consequently, according to this medical view of things, older women were likely to be carrying around inside them an excess of poisonous fluid which, when heated to boiling point by the action of hatred or envy, exhales toxic fumes through the eyes and then poisons susceptible people, particularly very young children because of their relative inability to resist it.

Signora Codronchi therefore connected the prettiness of her daughter with the envy or hatred of some elderly woman and made the natural deduction that such a woman would have been the source of a *veneficium*, an act of poisonous magic.

It is sometimes suggested that medieval and later Latin did not really distinguish between its various words for harmful magic, and that these may therefore be translated as 'witchcraft' and their operators as 'witches' without the need to elicit distinctions. Close reading of the various texts, however, does not altogether support this notion. *Maleficium* was an inclusive term for any type or act of magic which did and was intended to do harm, and included the use of incantations or spoken magical formulae which clearly did not involve poisonous substances. *Veneficium*, by contrast, as the Papal doctor Paolo Zacchia tells us, means some harm or injury projected towards somebody because of hatred, anger or envy, either by a look or by touch or by a word, or by the operation of a demon, or by the medium of poisons, or simply by a combination of these (*Quaestiones medico-legales* Book 2, title 2, question 13). Now, *veneficium* is based on the word for poison (*venenum*), a word which stands in need of qualification. Paolo Grillando, an early sixteenth-century priest and Papal judge, explains. 'There are several kinds or types of poisons, some of which are called "bad" (i.e. those which are made with a view to killing someone), and those known as "good" or "not bad" (i.e. which are made to cure a sick body, to assist conception, the so-called "poison to induce love", or anything else made for any other purpose, as long as it is not meant to kill)' (*De sortilegiis*, question 12). In other words, *venenum* had one sense quite close to the English 'drug', and so *veneficium* tends to imply an act which involves the use of substances which might have a beneficial or a maleficent effect according to intention or composition. But when one of these, for example the 'poison to induce love' (*venenum amatorium*), was administered in food or drink, it might be difficult for the magician to gauge the strength of its constituent materials, and if these were in any way toxic and death or severe illness resulted, onlookers might find it difficult to judge whether the sufferer had been deliberately or accidentally poisoned.

Cardano expressed the nature of *veneficia* when he said that they 'differ little from poisons' and went on to point out that the various materials which might go into their composition – human waste products (such as urine), blood, bits of hair, a dead person's bones, semen, needles, fragments of dead people's clothing, and so forth – and a description of the making of witches' maleficent 'powder' (specifically called 'poison') at a Sabbat in 1670 tells us that it consisted of a child's brains mixed with toads' ashes, and women's milk and urine, and that this was thrown over crops and into puddles whereby a thick fog was created and the crops were harmed. A woman who practised *veneficium* was thus a *venefica*, and Sennert tells us quite simply that '*veneficae* are so called because they make use of bad, poisonous substances [because "poisons", like "drugs", are interpreted with both a good sense and a bad], and do harm to people with them' (*Practica medicina* Book 6, part 9, chapter 2).

An elderly woman, then, perhaps fuelled by envy or hatred, her veins filled with boiling menstrual blood, had given off noxious fumes in an act of *veneficium*, and since the word *veneficium* could also suggest a collection of bizarre and nauseating objects devoted to producing harm, it is not surprising that Codronchi and his wife decided to search Francesca's cot, and neither would they have been surprised (however alarmed and frightened) to discover the kind of things they found. But this sinister gallimaufry was not the only thing suggested to Codronchi by the unfolding drama of his daughter's illness. The *veneficium* which was its source must have been caused by something – the *venefica* was merely the agent who acted on behalf of the source of actual power – and indeed Codronchi had no doubt at all that Satan was behind it. '*Veneficium*', he said, 'is caused by an evil spirit exercising his power after a human has entered into a pact with him because this human is intent on fulfilling some shameless, unprincipled desire of his or her own' (*De morbis veneficis* Book 3, chapter 1). How does the demon do this? According to Martin Del Rio, by separating from the blood 'spirits' (non-material essences similar in a way to air), which will then act as pathways for the disease. These then extract the essential poisonousness from the poisonous substances which make up the *veneficium*, and so become infected with this extracted toxicity, and then re-introduce themselves into the body, after which they can begin their deadly work. It sounds remarkably as though Satan and his minions might choose to operate as a type of lethal chemists, and indeed Del Rio likens part of this process to that of alchemy.

Having found magical instruments and having thought of evil spirits, Codronchi then called in an exorcist to give him advice and to oversee Francesca's cure. Yet he was a professional doctor. Some of her symptoms, at least, seemed to lie within his purvue. So why did he not try to cure her himself with natural rather than supernatural remedies? Or, if he thought natural medicine would be inefficacious, why did he not, in addition to exorcism, try counter-magic which would have been in the hands of a competent magician, male or female? As a good Catholic, of course, Codronchi may have been unwilling to enlist a help officially frowned on by the Church; but it is also possible that he simply distrusted many of the methods employed by unwitchers. Many of these actually seem to have been fairly harmless. On 3 June 1649 Janet Ross found herself before the kirk session of Belhavie on a charge of charming. It appeared she had tried to cure someone sick of a fever by administering a drink consisting of egg mixed with aquavitae and pepper. One is puzzled by this, until one remembers that the drink may have been accompanied by a spoken or whispered formula which could be interpreted as rendering the whole operation magical. Thus, on 3 July 1659, Donald Gilbertson gave Isobel Skeall in Canisbay a wristband of red thread which she wound about her upper arm while Donald spoke some words by way of a charm. But unwitchers were not the only people to use counter-magic in cases of illness. The German physician Paracelsus (1493–1541) tells us that some doctors were perfectly prepared to engage in cures which smack almost entirely of magic rather than medicine:

> Let the doctor make a wax image in the likeness of the patient and in the patient's name. Let him shape a small piece of wax so that it looks like the affected part, and with unwavering faith and a strong imagination let him believe he can restore health to the sick person by these means. At length, after he has said some short magical prayers, let him throw the small wax image on the fire. But if by chance he fears that the patient's life is in danger because of the severity of the pain or because of the way part of the body has been affected, let the doctor murmur certain words and burn the whole image, and the sick person is set free from the illness.
>
> (quoted by Del Rio)

If Codronchi was not prepared to get mixed up in this kind of thing, he may also have been wary of the way exorcists were equally happy to try medicine as part of their treatment. Indeed, he makes a strong plea against it, regarding exorcists' use of emetics and purges as a dangerous, rash intrusion by amateurs upon the professional doctor's field of expertise. 'So it will be better for the patient if exorcists abstain from cures based on medicine', he says, 'and consult physicians who will furnish appropriate remedies which, when fortified with holy blessings by the exorcists, will be able to cure the sick safely' (*De morbis veneficis* Book 4, chapter 4). Even baths and fumigations, also favoured by exorcists, he said, should be administered under medical supervision.

Categories which to us are distinct were not so regarded by people in earlier times. Doctors used magic, exorcists used medicines, magical practitioners combined religious formulae with curative or poisonous substances. But such fluidity does not imply that people were not prepared to take care in their assessments. The preface to the Catholic ritual of exorcism issued by Paul V in June 1614, for example, offers the priest a clear monition: 'Don't assume without hesitation that someone has been obsessed by an evil spirit. Look for those signs which distinguish an obsessed person from someone suffering from black bile [melancholia] or some other disease'. We have already noted the theory that spiritual or psychological disturbance had its origins in physical imbalance of the humours, especially the overproduction of black bile. Daniel Sennert gives us the medical explanation.

When many people have an over-abundance of the melancholy-humour but are not actually mad, delirium is not generated unless this humour communicates itself to the brain and dark, melancholy 'spirits' [in Del Rio's sense of the word] are added therefrom. This happens because of a person's mental state, an inclination to melancholy, worries, anxiety, all of which drive the humour into the brain. But sometimes demons, with God's permission, seize their opportunity, conjoin themselves to this physical condition, and feed the person with all kinds of sad, ridiculous, and depraved thoughts. This is why the popular name for melancholia is 'the Devil's bath'.

(*Practica Medicina* Book 1, part 2, chapter 11)

The Calvinist minister François Perreaud likened the process to the effect of smoke on a chimney-wheel. Usually the wheel does not move, but when a fire is lit underneath, it sends up smoke and vapours which cause the wheel to turn (*Demonologie* chapter 7). Melancholia or depressive illnesses, possession or obsession, and a range of wasting diseases might therefore have natural or demonically induced or assisted causes. It was generally recognised that even experts might have difficulty in telling the one cause from the other, although Paolo Zacchia says that the law distinguished between melancholics who exhibit the symptoms of depression, madness or delirium, and demoniacs who, as the name suggests, are under the influence of demonic activity, not to mention 'fanatics', 'lymphatics', 'enthusiasts', and several other categories of sufferers from corruption or disturbance of the humours, all of whom were likely to be regarded as demon-possessed in popular, not to say ignorant, usage (*Quaestiones medico-legales* Book 2, title 1, questions 9 and 18). But however nice the distinctions made by lawyers and expert physicians, it was still agreed that natural illnesses could be treated at least in part by magical methods, just as demonic afflictions could be treated in part by natural medicines, and that both were always susceptible to the aid of religion; and should demons be at the root of the trouble, it was wise to look for their human agents, witches, who through malefice or *veneficium* (their methods varied), provided the conduit whereby evil spirits could manifest their power and hatred.

But this cast of mind, apparently hostile to witches or *veneficae*, also provided the makings of a moral, if not a legal, defence. The way it worked was this. Purely medical treatments of the condition varied considerably, but often included use of strong, bitter substances which could be (and were) called 'poisons' and which, in the hands of a suspect witch rather than an accredited doctor, would have been called *veneficium*. Thus, for example, the German physician Felix

Platter (1536–1614) responded to the case of a young fellow-doctor who was convinced he had a frog living inside his guts, with medicines consisting of absinthe, olive oil, gentian, cumin, oil of peach, oil of bitter almond, and pills made of mercury. (No wonder Codronchi hesitated to use 'natural' remedies on his daughter.) Now, Platter's case is interesting because it points to an argument which was often used in discussions of witches and witchcraft: the notion that the suspects might be suffering from delusions rather than actually taking part in the more extravagant scenes – the flight, the Sabbat, the acts of fealty to Satan – which appear in many of their confessions. Modern commentators have been quick to seize upon this aspect of the subject and eager to attribute diabolic possession to ergot poisoning, or descriptions of the flight to the Sabbat to ingredients included in the ointments smeared upon the bodies of many witches prior to their magical journey. Early modern scholars, however, were not so simple as to imagine that there might be a single explanation for a complex phenomenon, and were perfectly well aware that certain herbs might induce hallucinations. Giambattista Della Porta, for example, mentioned in his *Magia Naturalis* (1589) references to a concoction which seems to have included mandrake, belladonna and henbane:

> When I was a youth, I tested this on the men with whom I was sharing a room. Their madness began to direct itself towards what they had been eating earlier, and they started to see images derived from the type of food they had eaten. One man who had gorged himself on beef hallucinated cattle bearing down on him with their horns, and other things of that kind. Another man drank one of these preparations, threw himself on the ground, and began to swim for his life, moving his arms and legs as though he were on the point of drowning; but when the strength of the drug began to grow weak, he started to squeeze his hair and clothes, like a shipwrecked mariner who had escaped from the sea.
>
> (Book 8, chapter 2)

Hallucinatory drugs apart, melancholia, however it was to be interpreted medically or legally, also afforded some people an explanation
for witches' confessions, although here again we must be careful not to
overestimate what these writers are saying. Reginald Scot is one of the
best-known of these 'sceptics'. 'Some of these melancholike persons
imagine they are witches and by witchcraft can worke woonders, and
doo what they list... This melancholike humor (as the best physicians
affirme) is the cause of all their strange, impossible and incredible confessions... If our witches' phantasies were not corrupted, nor their wils
confounded with this humor, they would not so voluntarilie and read-
ilie confesse that which calleth their life in question; whereof they
could never otherwise be convicted' (*Discoverie of Witchcraft* Book 3,
chapters 9 and 11). Pointed though this defence may seem, it is worth
noting that the kind of witchcraft Scot is discussing here involves the
extravagances of the Sabbat, not the far more common curative magic,
malefice, divination, or making of amulets, which constituted the
great bulk of magicians' (and therefore witches') activity throughout
Europe. So Scot and the others who similarly directed their fire on the
prosecutors of witches were, to an extent modern commentators
sometimes forget, blasting away at a relatively limited target, and drawing attention to an explanation their contemporaries were already
investigating and analysing in tremendous detail.

So, could suspect witches offer melancholia as a defence if they
were brought to trial? It seems not. In those courts whose procedures
allowed the accused to propone a defence, the arguments usually
rested on legal technicalities such as the admissibility of parts of the
evidence because of the omission of key words or phrases in individual items of the indictment – a frequent line taken by defence-advo-
cates in Scotland, for example – while submissions that certain acts
could be explained by reference to natural causes rather than witchcraft tended to be ignored or dismissed. Nor did legal distinctions
between melancholics, demoniacs and so forth necessarily help the
accused. A German jurisconsult, Benedict Carpzov (1595–1666),
argued that while people mad through delirium might not be responsible for their actions (although they should not on that account be set

free, but kept chained and locked up for their own and others' good), those mad through melancholia 'being people of a mind divided and dislodged, fabricating and telling themselves things which are preposterous, gloomy, bitter and hostile, are not entirely out of their minds and in consequence understand what they do and do it willingly and with malice' (*Practicae novae* Part 3). A witch therefore knew what she or he was doing. If she was in partnership with an evil spirit, she was culpable; if she practised fraud upon her clients, she was self-evidently culpable; and if she was melancholic, she was not so ill that she was unaware of her actions. So 'not guilty' verdicts – and one must remember that there were many of them – rested upon considerations other than medical theory or observation.

From all this, then, we are led to draw a number of conclusions. First, doctors were as likely to accept the reality of magic, whether in its beneficent or harmful mode, as anyone else, and many were prepared to use it in their treatments. Secondly, they were often called in to assist in the identification of a witch by looking for her or his mark and, of course, they attended those possessed by evil spirits, on which occasions they usually worked in tandem with exorcists whose efforts they complemented. Churchmen and doctors alike were alive to the possibility that certain manifestations of unusual or extreme behaviour, accompanied by physical symptoms well known to any who had dealings with diabolically inspired illnesses, might be caused or at least assisted by melancholia, a condition produced by an excess of black bile in the body, which could be used by evil spirits to introduce sickness and further a patient's mental and physical deterioration.

But doctors and churchmen also knew perfectly well that some cases they were called in to examine were fraudulent. Wier, for example, gives more than one account of feigned diabolical possession, although we must bear in mind that he was telling them as part of the anti-Catholic polemic which accompanies his work on witches (*De praestigiis daemonum* Book 4, chapters 27 and 28). Still, just because he had an agenda does not necessarily mean he was not pointing to a genuine phenomenon. In 1598, a French woman, Marthe Brossier, accused her neighbour Anne Chevreau of causing her to be possessed, and the accusation immediately set in train an extraordinary chain of events which led to Marthe's being, for nearly a year and a half, one of the most famous women in France, her case coming to the attention of the Paris Parlement itself. The documentation which accrued therefrom, however, suggests (and suggested to her contemporaries, including the unfortunate Anne) that she was a complex character, much beset by personal troubles, who had taken a conscious decision to behave like a demoniac, in which objective she was aided by her family because 'she would be pitied and onlookers would excuse rather than condemn her for her faults'. Thus began her remarkable career as a possessed woman; for she started to travel around the diocese of Orléans, demonstrating her possession to the ecclesiastical authorities and anyone else who cared to come and watch. She was exorcised over and over again, her performances acting on the one hand as morality plays – the demons were always expelled and so Good always triumphed over Evil – and on the other as confessional propaganda, showing to French Protestants the superior power of the Catholic priesthood. Finally, however, on 3 April 1599 she was arrested on a charge of fraud and imprisoned, and while in prison was obliged to submit to medical observation. The doctors were dismissive. Her 'possession', they said, arose from nothing more than a combination of duplicity and a little genuine illness.

None of this rattled belief either in the existence of evil spirits, of course, or in their power to do harm to humans if God so permitted. Indeed, the very existence of fraud tended to imply that, behind the deceit and the gullibility a competent or well-executed deception inspired, the reality of unseen worlds and preternatural entities was thereby merely illustrated further. In the end, Codronchi himself entertained no doubts on the subjects, as one of his final comments on his daughter's illness shows: 'Perhaps God permitted the *veneficium* so that I might experience in my own daughter something to which I used to give too little credit when it happened to other people'.

4

PATRICK MORTON: THE PROBLEMS OF DEMONIC POSSESSION

Witchcraft and possession are two distinct phenomena, although they are frequently confused because it was often the habit of sufferers to attribute their condition to the malevolence of a witch or a number of witches. Possession and obsession are also different phenomena (although in neither situation is a witch necessarily involved). John Bullokar defined the latter thus: 'A man is said to be obsest, when an evill spirit followeth him, troubling him divers times and seeking oportunitie to enter into him' (*An English Expositor*, 1616). Obsession refers to assault from outside. Possession, on the other hand, implies that the human has been taken over by an evil spirit which therefore lodges or operates from within. However, it is possible that a spirit might be persuaded or induced by a witch to take up residence in a human (or perhaps a creature such as a domestic animal), the object of the witch's request being to see the victim suffer both physical and spiritual pain. Therefore, possession may be a result of a non-material entity's endeavouring to accommodate itself within the unnatural medium of flesh and bone, and obsession may result from the sufferer's realisation during periods of quietness that her or his soul has been placed in jeopardy by the thoughts and words and actions she or he is forced to have and say and do during fits and spasms.

Conditions need to be favourable for the demon to gain entrance, of course. Possession does not happen willy-nilly. Let us therefore look at one or two cases to see if they have anything in common, or if a pattern begins to emerge. We shall start with the small fishing port of Pittenweem in Scotland. Kirk session records show that the towns-folk were happy to consult magical specialists about a number of specific personal problems. In January 1693 Margaret Greenhorn, a servant, was referred to the presbytery for 'consulting a man about things lost'. We do not know what, if anything, happened at the presbytery, but the experience of being referred seems to have had little effect since Margaret was cited to the session again in January 1698 after several reports of her bad carriage (behaviour), and there asked by the minister if it was true she had gone to consult a wizard about lost property. She replied that it was indeed, and that she had gone to him at the behest of her mistress. The expected public rebuke followed. In May, 1697 Agnes Adamson came before the session 'for consulting David Reddie… anent some cloaths which she pretended [claimed] were stollen from her', and here the record adds the interesting observation that, in choosing to appoint Agnes to be rebuked publicly the next Lord's Day, the session bore in mind 'how common this scandalous sin is of consulting persons reputed sorcerers anent things secret or lost'.

But in April 1698 the first sign of Pittenweem's most notorious episode might have been glimpsed on the horizon: on the 15th, Jean Durkie appeared before the session accused of consulting a woman 'under an ill report' about her husband who was abroad, about whether he would come home or not. Jean denied the charge, but then on 5 May she confessed it was true and was sentenced to receive the usual public rebuke. Jean, however, took the decision badly and, we are told, 'did not only curse and swear, but cursed the minister and elders, and had this horrible expression, "God's curse come upon them!"' This reaction was typical of her. On 11 March 1703 she was cited again, this time for scolding and fighting; and then on 24 May 1704 she was brought in front of the session for having approached one Nicholas Lowson (a woman, not a man), with the following extraordinary request: 'O Nickolas! Learn me to be a witch, that I may be avenged on the magistrates for sending my husband to Flanders'.

The request is unusual in that Jean wanted to be able to effect her own magical revenge rather than rely on someone else to do it for her. But she could scarcely have chosen a worse time to make it, for her approach coincided with a ripple of arrests in the community. Accusations of bewitchment were being laid against several individuals, of whom Nicholas Lowson was one, and it was not long before she and five other women along with a man, Thomas Brown, found themselves imprisoned – probably in the church steeple, a common place of confinement in places which did not have a tolbooth – before being examined by the kirk session on 29 May. Four of them confessed they had made a pact with the Devil, renounced their baptism, and attended meetings along with a number of others whom they named. A major witchcraft incident seemed to have been uncovered, and so naturally the matter was referred to the presbytery where all the accused were examined in some detail, and their alleged magical activities further exposed. Jean Durkie, too, found herself in front of the ministers where her particular affair was added to the burgeoning scandal.

Of what did the scandal consist? We may discount the references to a pact with Satan and meetings with other witches. These amounted to little more than the repetition of judicial formulae which, comparatively speaking, scarcely featured in Scottish witchcraft trials before the signing of the National Covenant in 1638 and the subsequent Bishops' Wars, although they became common enough thereafter. The meat of the accusation lay elsewhere. In March 1704, it was alleged, sixteen-year-old Patrick Morton, the son of a Pittenweem blacksmith, annoyed Beatrix Laing, long reputed to be a witch, be refusing to make her some nails. Next day, while passing her house, he noticed a wooden vessel with some water and a fire-coal in it, and these he took to be a magical charm directed against him. At once, we are told, he became so weak that he had to take to his bed and there he lay for several weeks, becoming more and more emaciated as time passed. Then, at the beginning of May, he started to have fits. His body would distort itself into remarkable and unnatural positions and his tongue would be drawn back right into his throat. Even so, he was able to let people know the names of those he claimed were inflicting these magical torments on him – Nicholas Lowson, Beatrix Laing, Janet Cornfoot, Margaret Wallace, Isobel Adamson, Margaret Jack and Thomas Brown – and on 1 June, the minister and some of the elders, the town bailie and one of the town councillors were deputed by the kirk session to go to Edinburgh and ask for a special commission to have these persons arrested and tried for witchcraft.

Now, the common modern understanding of demonic possession has been much influenced by the film of William Blatty's novel *The Exorcist* in which two Jesuit priests attempt to free a girl from the terrifying manipulations of an evil spirit. The film and the subsequent imitations and parodies of it make much of spectacular and frightening effects, thereby dramatising a highly personal internal war between the individual and an invading evil spirit in such a way that it becomes externalised theatre whose histrionics engage the audience not only in a suspension of disbelief, willing or unwilling, but in an active participation in the struggle fought by the human and non-human principals. One of the most common of these theatrical displays recorded in earlier testimonies was the victim's vomiting objects he or she would not normally have eaten.

Thus, Johann Wier records that Meiner Clatsius had a servant, William, who had been troubled for fourteen years by an evil spirit. At first people thought he was merely ill; but at some point he consulted a priest who was a professional unwitcher (not the same as an exorcist – the unwitcher could be anyone with the ability to deal with the effects of someone else's act of hostile magic), and when the ensuing exorcism started, William's throat swelled and his face turned livid as though he were going to suffocate. He then began to vomit. The objects taken from his mouth included the flap from a shepherd's breeches, flintstones, little balls of thread, long strands of hair, needles, strips of cloth and a peacock's feather. William blamed an unknown woman he had met by chance one day. She had breathed on his face, he said, and thence came his demonic illness (*De praestigiis daemonum* Book 4, chapter 6). (One is reminded of the theory that menstruating women emitted poisonous vapours which had the power to corrode mirrors and infect any people they met.)

Another common symptom was the ability of the sufferer to twist his or her body into positions usually considered abnormal or impossible. For example, the trials of a twelve-year-old boy, Thomas Harrison, were described by an eye-witness who took notes on his condition and wrote them up afterwards.

By his torments he was brought so low, weak, and feeble, that he was almost nothing but skin and bones, yet for the space of four and twenty hours every day (having only one half hour respite, which they called his awakening time, and wherein they gave him a little food) he was of that extraordinary strength, that if he foulded his hands together, no man could pull them asunder: if he rolled his head, or tossed his whole body (as usually he did) no man could stay, or restrain him: he would, to the great astonishment of the hearers, howl like a dog, mew like a cat, roar like a bear, froth like a boar: when any prayed with him, his passions were strongest, and his rage and violence greatest, ready to fly in their faces, and to drown their voices by his yellings, and out-cries: if one came near him with a Bible, though under his cloak, and never so secret, he would run upon him, and use great violence to get it from him, and when he could get any, he rent them in pieces: sometimes he would lie along, as if he had been stark dead, his colour gone, and his mouth so wide open, that he would on a sudden thrust both his hands into it: and notwithstanding his great weakness, he would leap and skip from his bed to the window, from the window to the table, and so to bed again, and that with such agility, as no tumbler could do the like. And yet all this while his legs were grown up so close to his buttocks, so that he could not use them: sometimes we saw his chin drawn up to his nose, that his mouth could scarce be seen: sometimes his chin and forehead drawn almost together like a bended bow.

(Samuel Clarke: *The Second Part of the Marrow of Ecclesiastical History*, 1675, Book 2, pp. 94–5)

Blatty's novel was based on an incident reported in the *Washington Post* on 20 August 1949. A fourteen-year-old boy, it said, had been taken over by some kind of demon which made him maniacally enraged and obscene, altered his voice and face, and caused red welts forming letters and numbers to appear on his body. Now, Dr Balthasar Han, principal physician to the Elector of Saxony at the beginning of the seventeenth century, had a patient who exhibited some of these same symptoms, too. His account is summarised by a younger contemporary, the American pastor Increase Mather.

> In November 1634, she was, to the amazement of all spectators, pricked and miserably beaten by an invisible hand, so as that her body from head to foot was wounded as if she had been whipped with thorns. Sometimes a perfect sign of the cross was imprinted on her skin; sometimes the usual configurations whereby astronomers denote the caelestial bodies such as Mars and Jupiter and their conjunctions and oppositions; and the characters used by chymists [i.e. alchemists] (in which sciences, though that be not usual for those of her sex, she was versed). These characters would remain for several weeks after the invisible hand had violently impressed them on her body; also a needle was thrust into her foot, which caused it to bleed. Once she took the needle and put it into the fire; and then an old woman, to whom she had given some of her wearing linnen, appeared to her with a staff in her hand, striking her with a cruel blow, and saying, 'Give me my needle'.
>
> *(Providences in New England*, 1684, chapter 6)

So far, then, a pattern of sorts does seem to be emerging. The victim is young; the possession takes its toll on the sufferer's physical strength, and yet her or his fits include violent dramas both upon and by the body; religion in whatever form it shows itself is rejected: in a word, the victim displays every symptom of moral and physical chaos. Family, priests, doctors and spectators would need to try to make sense of this. Welts on the body, for example, if caused by an evil spirit, might be considered similar to those insensible points or fleshly excrescences known as witches' marks, a very strong indication that Satan or one of his agents was involved in the phenomenon; and physical distortions could not only have reminded people of the normal contortions attendant on infirmities such as fever or tetanus, but would have told onlookers that invasion of a corporeal being by a non-material entity was bound to inflict tension and suffering as two incompatible forms of existence were thrust together. Visions of the person causing the symptoms of possession were also significant, for if they were visions of identifiable human beings, these originators could be arrested and charged with malign magic, and once that had happened experience suggested the possession and its torments would cease.

The priests called in to exorcise the afflicted, however, saw their first and principal task as engaging the demon or demons in extended verbal exchanges rather than immediately expelling them from the patient. This is perfectly logical. Rather like a modern physician who must first identify the cause of an illness – virus, bacterium, germ, bacillus, and so forth – before prescribing treatment, so before expelling a demon the exorcist must know its name, its rank, its condition, its appointed task, its locality within the sufferer and its proper abode within the other world. Thus, in the famous case of multiple possession in the Ursuline convent of Loudun in 1634, the Mother Superior was found to have several possessing demons: Leviathan, belonging to the order of *Seraphim*, who was lodged in the middle of her forehead; Aman, belonging to the order of *Powers*; Isacaron, also one of the *Powers*, lodged below the last rib on her right side; Balam, one of the *Dominions*, lodged in the second rib on her right; Asmodeus, one of the *Thrones*; and Behemoth, again one of the *Thrones*, lodged in her stomach. Now, the demons would not surrender their names without a struggle. Once known, they could be expelled by various powers resident in divine names and by the impulsive forces inherent in the recitation of sacred histories, such as Christ's redemption of humankind, all of which laid bare to the demon itself its impotence in the presence of mediated heavenly power, and its mistake in taking up residence in a place other than that destined for it by God. Treating the demon as though it were both malicious and confused, therefore, presented the exorcising priest with an extremely complex problem. Hence the length of so many exorcisms, and the necessity to repeat them because the demon had either not been expelled, or had been unable to find his way to his proper abode and had thus returned to the last place he knew – the human being.

In some cases, however, certain aspects of possession might look very much like a simple physical illness. Jean Fernel (1497–1558), a French philosopher and mathematician turned doctor, records one such instance. A young man of good family was given to bouts of violent shaking and convulsion. Sometimes only a part of his body, such as a finger or arm or leg, would be affected; and sometimes his tremors were so violent that it took four servants to hold him down. These seizures happened at least ten times a day, leaving him exhausted, although his speech, mind and senses seemed to be unimpaired by the ferocity of his convulsions. Doctors were called in and came to the conclusion that the problem was akin to epilepsy, but not epilepsy itself. They administered a wide range of remedies: frequent clysters, purges of every kind, cupping-glasses, soothing ointments and plasters, all intended to counteract the malignant, poisonous vapour diagnosed as the cause of his affliction. When these did no good, the doctors tried sweat-baths and a decoction of guiac; but still the illness did not yield to their efforts.

Finally it became clear that this was a case of demonic possession. There were various indicative signs (all of which were commonly observable in demoniacs): the sufferer was able to speak Greek, a language he did not know; he revealed personal secrets of the doctors who were attending him; he laughed at their efforts to treat him; whenever his father tried to visit him, he would object violently, shouting, 'Keep him out! Drive him away!', and would beg people to remove the image of Saint Michael from a chain round his neck. If anyone spoke sacred words in his hearing, he would counter them with profanities, becoming alternately more fiercely agitated and then as stiff as a board. At last, exorcisms began. The demon was asked his name, by what means he troubled the sufferers, and by what or whose authority. He answered that he situated himself in various parts of the young man's body, and that during those times when the patient was at rest, he migrated into other people. As for his authority, the demon said he had been sent into this particular body by someone whose name he would not reveal (*De abditis rerum causis* [1548], Book 2, chapter 16). So, what may have begun as apparent epilepsy revealed itself, through signs well-known at least to those called in to deal with it, as a maleficent spirit-invasion whose remedy required the combined efforts of both doctors and priests, the former to treat the physical symptoms produced by the spiritual illness, the latter to get to grips with and expel the malign force at the heart of the problem.

One may note that not every case of possession involves an act of witchcraft. For that to be established, the answer to the exorcist's question, 'Who is causing this condition?', must include the name of at least one human being who is thereby designated not as the actual cause (which is the presence of a demon), but as the agent of that cause; and Fernel's youth seems to come near this point when he exhibits fear at the sight of his father, although Fernel gives no indication that the father was ever named or prosecuted as a guilty party. But naming or indicating someone human and living as a principal in the case is, of course, a situation which may lend itself to fraud, as people in earlier times were well aware.

In 1597–98, for example, twenty-year-old William Somers exhibited several startling features of possession; a large soft lump the size of an egg seemed to run along his leg and thence into various parts of his body; he had bouts of extraordinary strength, underwent great facial distortion and bodily contortions, remained unhurt when he fell into a fire, revealed things which had been done in his absence, and spoke in strange tongues. He blamed an old woman whom he met by chance at a coalpit. She asked him where he lived and whither he was going and, after demanding money, made him eat a piece of bread which proved to be the means whereby a demon made its way inside his body. As William Dragge observed, 'Sometimes they make natural Remedies to produce preternatural Effects; as by giving the party somewhat to eat, but that that is eaten hath no power to raise such strange Symptomes, but rather gives power to the Witch, by giving any to, or receiving any thing from the party that is to be bewitched; and until then, some Witches have confessed that they could not have their minds, or power to bewitch' (*Daimonomageia*, 1665). A few years later, in the autumn of 1604, another twenty-year-old, Anne Gunter, began to display symptoms of possession – vomiting pins, violent shaking and contortions of her body, and the ability to disclose information about people, which should have been secret or unknown to her in advance. Both cases, however, were fraudulent. Somers confessed as much, and Anne Gunter was shown to have collaborated with her father in what would nowadays be called a 'scam'.

It is notable that Anne blamed individuals for her fits: Elizabeth Gregory, a woman unpopular in the locality; Agnes Pepwell, who was reputed to be a witch; and Agnes's illegitimate daughter, Mary. Agnes ran away, but Elizabeth and Mary were arrested and put on trial. Fortunately they were acquitted, but we can see reason behind Anne's naming of them. Elizabeth was chosen as the principal culprit because her husband and Anne's father were at feud; Agnes's reputation marked her out as a convenient possible scapegoat; and Mary was tainted both by her relationship to Agnes and by her own illegitimacy. She was not 'respectable' either in her birth or in her family and could therefore serve as a named target for social opprobrium. One of the most significant features of her case – significant both to modern eyes and to those of her contemporaries – was her confession that she had modelled many of her fits and trances upon those contained in a lengthy pamphlet entitled *The most strange and admirable discoverie of the three witches of Warboys arraigned, convicted, and executed at the late assizes of Huntingdon* (1593), a copy of which was found in the Gunters' house. The Warboys case was fairly straightforward. The victims were the children of a well-to-do middle-class couple, the Throckmortons; the alleged witches who had caused their possession were members of a local farming family. The pamphlet says the victims were children, but this does not mean that they were all especially young; Joan Throckmorton, the oldest, for example, was about nineteen. Their fits took the form of 'epileptic' convulsions which the sufferers blamed on one Alice Samuel. It is worth remarking that these fits went on for well over three years during which time the victims' parents did little more than to ask Alice Samuel to confess her witchcraft and remove the bewitchment, a quiet endurance on both sides which mirrors the periods frequently of considerable length – ten, twenty, thirty years – that a witch could remain known and active in her or his community without being prosecuted. The pamphlet's long descriptions of the children's fits seem to have been taken from court records and later printed as part of its narrative. Anne Gunter therefore had plenty of material on which to base her domestic and public performances.

Interestingly enough, this situation is paralleled by the case of Patrick Morton from Pittenweem. As we have seen, he appeared to be subject to fits which were diagnosed as demonically inspired, and he named several people as the causes or agents of his suffering. The affair was considered so serious that it went from the local presbytery to the General Assembly of the Church of Scotland, and thence to the Privy Council which was asked for a commission to try Beatrix Laing and her co-conspirators. The Council considered the request and sent three men, including the Lord Advocate himself, to Pittenweem to investigate the case where, after diligent inquiry, they decided not to proceed with any prosecution and gave instructions that all the accused were to be released. The women were duly set free. Thomas Brown, however, had died while in prison. The women Patrick had accused may have been set at liberty, but their trials were by no means over. Emotions in Pittenweem were running high, and Beatrix Laing continued to be persecuted by the townsfolk who first of all imprisoned her for five months and then, when she escaped, prevented her from returning to her house. The Council's records make disturbing reading:

> The petitioner was thrown into the tolbooth of Pittenweem by the minister and magistrats thereof; and because she would not confess that she was a witch and in compact with the devill, was tortured by keeping her awake without sleep for fyve days and nights together, and by continually pricking her with instruments in the shoulders, back and thighs, that the blood gushed out in great abundance, so that

her lyfe was a burden to her; and they urging her continuallie to confess, the petitioner expressed several things as they directed her, to be
rid of the present torture; and because she afterwards avowed and
publicly told that what she had said to them of her having seen the
divell, etc. was lies and untruths, they putt her in the stocks for several
dayes, and then carried her to the thief's hole, and from that they
transported her to a dark dungeon, wher she was allowed no maner of
light, nor humane converse; and in this condition she lay for fyve
months together; and at last, having found means to get out of the said
dungeon, she wandered about in strange places in the extremity of
hunger and cold, though, she thanked God, she had a competency at
home, but dared not come near her own house, because of the fury
and rage of the people.

(*RPC* 1 May 1705)

She was thus forced to live as a beggar, during which time she somehow managed to get a complaint to the Privy Council. Her petition
did her little good, however. Pittenweem Burgh records note that 'the
Lords required that the bailies and council should engage in a bond to
protect the said Beatrix Laying against any rabble should assault her;
which they unanimously refused to do in respect she may be mur-
thered in the night without their knowledge' (11 May 1705). So they
sat on their hands, and the Privy Council failed to pursue the matter
further.

One may ask why the representatives of the Privy Council had
ordered Beatrix and the others to be released after their first investigation. The answer may be that certain aspects of Patrick Morton's story
are reminiscent of the notorious Bargarran case. This involved an
eleven-year-old girl, Christian Shaw, who during the second half of
1697 displayed many of the classic symptoms of demonic possession
and accused a total of twenty-one persons of bewitching her. Seven of
these were executed on 10 June the following year, and with their
deaths her symptoms first faded then ceased altogether. The case had
caused a great stir, with published accounts of it appearing in pamphlet form. So it comes as significant to find that the minister of

Pittenweem had been reading one of these to Patrick Morton while the boy lay in the midst of his 'magical' sickness. Why on earth should he have done such a thing? In view of his later brutality to Beatrix Laing, one asks oneself whether it may be he wanted to engineer the whole thing as a way of furnishing excuse to persecute her and perhaps the others for reasons of his own. There is no proof that such was his intention, but the fact that Patrick did not begin to exhibit signs of demonic possession until half-way through his illness may be treated as potentially suspicious. Were the two of them colluding? It is at least possible.

But it would be too facile, and too insulting to the intelligence of those concerned either as participants or onlookers, to suggest that all cases of possession were no more than fraud supported by greed for money or prestige on the one hand, and superstitious credulity on the other. Apart from any other considerations of historical ethics, it begs the question, what does one mean by fraud in such a context? Let us take the example of Mercy Short, aged seventeen, a servant living in Boston, Massachusetts. In the summer of 1692, she was sent to the local gaol and there encountered Sarah Good, one of the imprisoned witches from Salem. Sarah asked her for tobacco, but Mercy refused, throwing a handful of wood-shavings in Sarah's face with the contemptuous remark, 'That's tobacco good enough for you!' Not long after (the same night, in fact), she had a fit which lasted for several weeks, during which she exhibited many of the symptoms then regarded as typical of possession. Cotton Mather, one of the ministers who was taking a particular interest in the similar outbreaks of witch-induced possession in Salem, devoted a great deal of his time to freeing Mercy from the grip of the demon, and throughout the winter of 1692–93 held what amounted to revivalist meetings in her bedroom, all the while making extensive notes on her case, which remained in manuscript until they were published as *A Brand Pluck'd Out of the Burning* in 1914.

Now, two years previously, when Mercy was fifteen, she had been captured by Indians who killed her family and carried her off to Canada where she stayed until she was redeemed along with other prisoners and brought back to Boston. Mather questioned her closely about what had been a very recent and very disturbing experience, and was told she had been much troubled by demons who had pinched her and bitten her and slashed her with knives. One of them she described as 'a Divel having the Figure of a Short and a Black Man... He was a wretch no taller than an ordinary Walking-Staff; he was not of a Negro, but of a Tawny, or an Indian colour; he wore a high-crowned Hat, with straight Hair; and had one Cloven-foot'. One is reminded of descriptions of the Devil as told by confessing witches in Western Europe. Apart from the cloven foot, which seems to be a gratuitous detail added, perhaps, in answer to a prompting by Mather, the picture of him as a composite dark-skinned man and fashionably-dressed gentleman can be found in many versions of meetings between Satan and witches, not at the Sabbat, but in the circumstances of everyday life – on the highway, on the sea-shore, in someone's house.

Mercy's answers to Mather's probing questions reveal not the carefully constructed narrative of a self-conscious fraud, but the frightened, almost dream-like responses of someone who is trying, with the help of a skilful interrogator, to exorcise from her own vividly-remembered experience the memory of real people whom contemporary fears and prejudices were encouraging her to regard as no better than devils. Only twenty years before, white soldiers had been massacring Indians – men, women and children alike – in accesses of hysterical rage. Many of those who flocked into Mary's room to witness her seizures and pray for her recovery would have been aware both of these hideous killings and of Mercy's captivity. But there is never any sense throughout the accounts of her long possession that she is playing upon those fears or memories. Her case does not end in any acknowledgement of deliberate deception, such as occurs in the cases of William Somers, Anne Gunter or Patrick Morton. So if Mercy and Cotton Mather were indeed engaged in constructing a case of possession (for which there is no evidence at all), they were doing so, not for gain or notoriety or revenge, but for interior motives unrealised by either and for goals unconsciously pursued; and if they were not conscious of perpetrating, who are we to impose deception upon them?

Demonic possession should be seen, in fact, as part of a broader spectrum of behavioural situations in which an individual or a group of individuals is invaded and taken over by some conscious force or forces, power or powers, entity or entities, which are other than human. Experiences such as these will include ecstatic religious rapture, shamanic trance, and invited possession, in which the human deliberately or involuntarily acts as a vessel for the intruding entity (of which the Pythia at Delphi or the Tibetan State Oracle are examples). How these and the experiences of demonic possession are interpreted depends on a wide variety of external factors – religion, politics, economics, culture, social expectation and so forth – and therefore interpretations are likely to mould, to a greater or lesser extent, the records of individual seizures, which then become referential evidence underpinning the interpretation of future incidents. Thus, for example, while demoniacs of the thirteenth century were reported as real people to whom real experiences had happened, the reporting was turned into a literature of edification to illustrate the power and the mercy of God working through the intercession of a saint or the Church, since the narrative invariably ended with the expulsion of the demon and the infliction of one more defeat upon the Devil. The nineteenth and twentieth centuries, by contrast, tended to seize upon the association of possession with physical or psychic illness allied to eccentric behaviour, and suggest an explanation couched purely in medical terminology, such as 'hysteria' or 'multiple personality'. Explaining historical phenomena in terms of one's own or one's culture's intellectual predilections has a limited value. It actually explains little or nothing about the historical episode itself which needs to be re-presented to a later audience in its own terms, so that insight may jump the years and a previous way of thinking be given its proper weight and appreciation.

There is another aspect of demonic possession which lends itself to being misunderstood. Apparently most demoniacs were female. The Middle Ages and early modern period had no difficulty in noting that women were, by their nature, both sexually rampant and morally frail, so it was small wonder that Satan would seize upon their weaknesses and manipulate them to his desires. What is more, women's bodies leaked, as was evident from lactation and menstruation. This extrusion of substances – and demoniacs' vomiting from within the body objects such as pins or coal or hair which were properly external to it seemed to confirm and emphasise the point – therefore meant that women's bodies were less self-contained than those of men, making the business of crossing their physical boundaries much easier. Several notorious episodes of possession among the nuns of a number of French convents during the seventeenth century might thus seem to provide both early and late modern commentators with explanations satisfactory to their separate cultural points of view. Religious women were obvious targets for Satan and so perhaps even more open to attack than their secular sisters; and the presence in convents of young women without a true vocation provided the psychological hothouse which might easily see relief, and rebellion against a stifling male authority, break out in the peculiar form of possession. The apparent absence of such outbreaks in male monasteries might be noted as supportingly suggestive.

But none of this is altogether satisfactory. Monasteries contained boys and young men without vocation, too, and it is a tendentious point which tries to align earlier derogation of women with latter-day psychologising. More importantly, we know there were male demoniacs as well as female (just as we know there were male witches as well as female), and any explanation which ignores them either deliberately or tacitly is omitting a necessary part of the whole. Perhaps the most significant point about waves of possession (as opposed to disparate single instances), is that they tended to be linked with expectations of the Apocalypse and the Last Judgement. It is a connection made over and over again during both the sixteenth and seventeenth centuries.

Thus, for example, the German Protestant minister Daniel Schaller,

1 *Ulrich Molitor,* De laniis et phitonicis mulieribus *(1489). Instructing Church and State in the ways of witchcraft.*

2 *Title-page to Martín Del Rio's* Disquisitiones Magicae. *It illustrates the protracted struggle between Moses and Pharaoh's magicians.*

3 *Paul Christian,* Histoire de la magie *(Paris, n.d.). Satan presiding at the Sabbat.*

4 *Jan Ziarnko's illustration of a witches' Sabbat,
specifically engraved to accompany the second edition of
Pierre de Lancre's* Tableau de l'inconstance des
mauvais anges et démons *(1613).*

5 *Angelo dei Gambilioni,* De maleficiis *(1526). A male
witch is interrogated and hanged.*

6 *Physician studying a specimen of urine brought from a patient by his servant who is holding the wicker case for the urine-bottle.*

7 *An example of the written pact between a priest (Urbain Grandier) and the Devil (c.1632). It is signed by Grandier and witnessed by six demons.*

8 *Christian Frommand,* Tractatus de fascinatione *(1674). The effects of the evil eye.*

9 *Title-page to Battista Codronchi's* De morbis veneficis.

10 *Cotton Mather.*

11 *Pierre Boaistuau*, Histoires Prodigieuses *(1597). A priest exorcising a demon from a possessed woman.*

12 *Pittenweem in 1877.*

13 *Kirk session entry relating to witches in* Pittenweem, 29 May 1704.

14 *Francesco-Maria Guazzo,* Compendium maleficarum *(1626). Satan marking a male witch.*

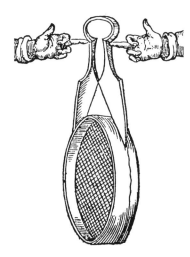

15 *George Pictorius,* Pantopilion *(1563). The sieve and shears. One of the magical methods of detecting thieves.*

16 *Swimming a witch, a nineteenth-century interpretation.*

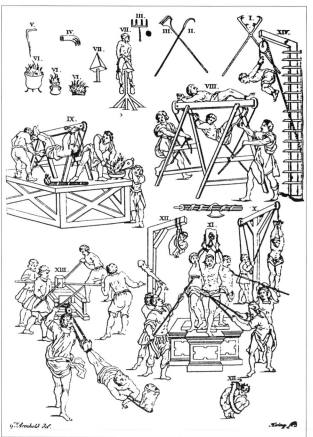

17 *Olaus Magnus,* Historia de gentibus septentrionalibus *(1555). A male and a female witch raising a storm at sea.*

18 *Christian Ulrich Grupen,* Observatio iuris criminalis de applicatione tormentorum *(Hanover, 1754). An illustration of the various methods and instruments of torture.*

Just as in the time of the first bodily coming of the Lord Christ to deliver and mediate for us, a great swarm and number of such wretched possessed folk was found everywhere; so there is no doubt that in these present times, the swarm and number of demoniacs is so great, both near and far, that it is a truly powerful and double proclamation that for the second and last time our dear Lord and true Saviour Jesus Christ will come.

(*Herolt*, 1595)

As signs of the end of the world, therefore, demoniacs were highly significant people, for the demons' voices issuing from their mouths were speaking from knowledge and experience not only other than human but greater, too. They engaged onlookers and exorcists in debates which took on extra urgency in the light of expectation that these were the Final Times; and while it was known that Satan is the great deceiver, if he (or his minions) could be forced by the exorcist to tell certain things truthfully, it was evident that in this instance he should be believed. So when he confessed his true name, he provided the preliminary means whereby effective exorcism could begin and the process of expulsion from the human body be initiated. So, too, when he named the human beings who were acting as his agents to bewitch the possessed individual, the priests and doctors who had diligently applied their specialist knowledge to the case and diagnosed a spiritual, not a physical, affliction would have been criminally negligent of the sufferer's welfare had they *not* sought out and arrested the culpable parties. For the denunciation of their guilt had surely come from an unimpeachable source.

5

JOHN KINCAID:
PROFESSIONAL WITCH-PRICKER

In the summer of 1597, the authorities in the central belt of Scotland made much use of one Margaret Atkin, a confessing witch, who claimed she was able to recognise witches at a glance. Such a useful talent was not to be left unexploited.

This Summer there was a great business for the triall of Witches; amongst others one *Margaret Atkin* being apprehended upon suspicion, and threatned with torture, did confess her self guilty. Being examined touching her associates in that trade, she named a few, and perceiving her delations finde credit, made offer to detect all of that sort, and to purge the Countrey of them, so that [on condition that] she might have her life granted; for the reason of her knowledge she said, *That they had a secret mark, all of that sort, in their eyes, whereby she could surely tell, how soon she lookt upon any whether they were witches or not*; and in this she was so readily believed, that for the space of 3 or 4 months she was carried from town to town to make discoveries in that kinde. Many were brought to question by her delations, especially at *Glasgow*, where divers innocent women, through the credulity of the Minister M. *John Cowper*, were condemned and put to death. In the end she was found to be a meer deceiver (for the same persons that the one day she had declared guilty, the next day being presented in another habit, she cleansed) and sent back to *Fife*, where first she was apprehended. At her triall she affirmed all to be false that she had confessed, either of her self or others, and persisted in this to her death: which made many forthink their too great forwardness that way, and moved the King [James VI] to recall the Commissions given out against such persons, discharging all proceedings against them, except in cases of voluntary confession, till a solid order should be taken by the Estates, touching the form that should be kept in their triall.[4]

The problem of fraud inherent in such claims was not confined to Scotland. A fourteen-year-old French boy, for example, was put to work in the Basque country in 1612 on the grounds that he could recognise witches by looking them straight in the eye; but under close questioning by a Jesuit priest who had been favourably inclined to him at first, the boy admitted he had been lying. During the same investigations, a sixteen-year-old boy, Pedro de los Reyes, had made similar claims, but here again there seems to have been enough suspicion of fraud to have him arrested and imprisoned while the ecclesiastical Tribunal considered how best to handle the case against him. One might think that teenage boys would be the last people anyone would want to use to identify witches, since the suspect's survival or death could, in practice, almost certainly rest in large part on such testimony. There was, however, a long magical tradition of employing young boys as mediums, although admittedly these tended to be younger than teenagers. The general practice was to pour oil into the child's palm and see (or let him see) what future events appeared in this makeshift mirror; and while it is true that these boy-mediums were supposed to be virgins, the tradition of their use might suggest that some of them retained a preternatural ability beyond the age of puberty. Caution, therefore, rather than outright dismissal would have seemed an appropriate reaction to any of their claims.

Recognising a witch by looking into her eyes was not, however, the most common or widespread method available. On 16 June 1661 in Dalkeith, Janet Paiston was being examined on charges of practising witchcraft:

The minister and bailie did send for John Kincaid in Tranent, the ordinary pricker and trier of such persons; and he being come for that
end, after he being charged upon his great oath that he should go
about his office faithfully, and therein do and declare nothing but
what was of truth, he found two marks upon her, which he declared
to be the Devil's marks: which indeed appeared so to be, in respect she
had nor sense nor feeling of the same when they were pricked, nor
could tell in what place of her body the same were.

(*JC* 26/27/9/22)

Of all the various means whereby people were tested to find out
whether or not they were witches, pricking is one of the best known.
A long pin was sunk into the flesh at many different parts of the body,
and should the suspect individual not cry out in pain, or should the
pierced spot fail to issue blood, a Devil's mark was thereby discovered,
a potent (though not necessarily conclusive) indication that the individual had met the Devil and had made a pact with him to become his
servant and so renounce God and Christian baptism. These curiosities
of the witch's condition were largely unknown or at least ignored
before the fifteenth century, but became popular forms of recognition
in the sixteenth and seventeenth centuries, perhaps as a result of growing interest in physiognomy, the study of marks and lines on the body,
and especially upon the face. Codronchi gives the standard account of
how they came to be impressed. Once the new witches had
renounced their baptism at a Sabbat, he wrote, 'the demon thrusts his
finger-nail into their forehead, pretending to scratch away their bap-
tismal oil and to obliterate the indelible mark [*stigma*] of their baptism... Then he imprints his mark [*stigma*] or stamp [*character*] on some
part of their body, particularly one which is concealed' (*De morbis veneficis* Book 3, chapter 4); and the Papal physician Zacchia notes further
that these marks appear to be insensible and bloodless. *Stigma*, he goes
on, is a word referring especially to a mark made with a hot iron or
scorching dyes, such as was used in ancient times to brand cattle and
tattoo slaves, thereby designating a creature or person the property of
his or her master. But the Devil cannot really excise or remove the

stigma of baptism, however much he tries, and 'just as no one is a Christian without baptism, and with baptism each person is a Christian: so no one without the stigma is a worker of magic, and a person found with the stigma is a worker of magic' (*Quaestiones medico-legales* Book 7, title 4, question 1).

The conception of a person's identity or status being indicated by some kind of outward sign was less odd to the earlier period than it may be to ours. In the late Middle Ages, for example, people were used to regarding clothes as identification markers – colour, cloth and texture were all social indicators. Knights wore devices on their shields, the religious military orders had distinctive crosses on their cloaks or habits, rattles were carried by lepers, stars and half-moons were worn by Jews and Muslims. Magical sigils were drawn or carved by magicians, which were intended to identify particular angels or spirits, or to act as protective identification marks as the magician rose through the angel- or demon-inhabited regions of the spirit during protracted ecstatic rituals. People also tattooed themselves with astrological or magical marks, the tattoos being both temporary and permanent. Professional magical curers in Italy, known as *Salvatori*, claimed to have the mark of a snake impressed on their flesh, a mark which gave them power over both serpents and poisons; and in spring 1609 the English physician and astrologer Simon Forman tattooed the planetary signs of Venus and Jupiter, along with the astrological sign of Cancer, on his left arm and right breast. Even God, according to a Coptic spell, has seven sacred vowels tattooed upon his chest, and during the Middle Ages Christians had themselves tattooed with the name of Jesus and other identificatory symbols of their faith. It would therefore have been very strange to contemporary opinion had witches *not* borne some kind of mark which would identify them as followers of Satan and foot-soldiers in his army.

Sometimes (as was the general rule in Scotland) the mark could be found on the arm or neck or shoulder, not especially 'hidden'; but elsewhere a suspect woman often had her head shaved – in itself a sign of shame or infamy, as can be seen from the case of alleged *collaboratrices* in France at the end of the Second World War. Thus, on 16 May

1658, Marguerite Touret was visited in prison by three surgeons who shaved her head, blindfolded her, and then proceeded to prick her head in several different places with their needles. On each occasion save one, Marguerite said she could feel the pain and told them where she felt it. The exception was a place on her skull about the size of a small coin, and when they pierced this Marguerite showed no discomfort, no matter how often or how deeply they drove the needle in. This indication that the surgeons had found a Satanic mark led to a fuller and more rigorous examination. They shaved her armpits and tested her as far as her waist. A second mark, the size of a small bean and whitish in colour, was discovered on her right groin. This was pierced to a depth of perhaps two inches, but Marguerite gave no sign she felt any pain. Finally, her whole body was shaved, but further testing found no more Devil's marks.

In England, women were employed to look in the privy parts of the female suspect's body for teat-like growths or similar blemishes which were accounted Devil's marks whence the witch's familiar-spirits were able to feed. The Essex witch-finder Matthew Hopkins wrote a pamphlet in 1647 at the very end of his career, describing his methods in answer to objections which been raised against them. In reply to the point that it was almost impossible to tell witches' teats and natural excrescences apart, he said (speaking of himself in both the first and the third person):

> The reasons in breefe are three, which for the present he judgeth to differ from naturall marks; which are:
> 1) He judgeth by the unusualness of the place where he findeth the teats in or on their bodies, being farre distant from any usuall place, from whence such naturall markes proceed, as if a witch plead the markes found are Emerods [haemorrhoids], if I finde them on the bottome of the back-bone, shall I assent with him, knowing they are not neere that veine, and so others by child-bearing, when it may be they are in the contrary part?
> 2) They are most commonly insensible, and feele neither pin, needle, aul, etc. thrust through them.

3) The often variations and mutations of these marks into severall formes, confirms the matter, as if a Witch hear a month or two before that the Witch-finder (as they call him) is comming, they will, and have put out their Imps to others to suckle them, even to their owne young and tender children; these upon search are found to have dry skinnes and filmes only, and be close to the flesh, keepe her 24 hours with a diligent eye, that none of her spirit come in any visible shape to suck her; the women have seen the next day after her Teats extended out to their former filling length, full of corruption ready to burst, and leaving her alone then one quarter of an houre, and let the woman go up againe, and shee will have them drawn by her Imps close again.

(*The Discovery of Witches*, 1647)

Discovery of such marks was very often, though not invariably, regarded as a sure sign that the suspect person was a witch. Jacques Fontaine, physician-in-ordinary to Louis XIII, certainly thought so and indeed was convinced that the mark alone provided irrefutable evidence of guilt, although he was aware that there were differences of opinion about this. With such dissent, however, he had little patience. 'They say it is difficult to distinguish [witches' marks] from a natural blotch, a boil, or a natural blemish, thereby clearly demonstrating that they are not good physicians' (*Des marques des sorciers*, 1611). Witches' marks, he went on, have no feeling and contain no serum: nor do they rise above the surface of the skin. Consequently, these spots on the body must be dead, rendered so by the Devil. But as to whether they can disappear once the suspect witch has been arrested, searched, pricked and interrogated, he was not so sure. Certainly this had happened in the case of witchcraft he was discussing in his pamphlet. The woman had been examined once by doctors and surgeons and the marks found; but then she had repented and, upon being examined a second time by doctors and surgeons, 'the marks they had found before no longer existed; for when they inserted a needle into them, as they had on the first occasion, they found that the place where the mark had been was very tender, and when the needle was withdrawn, dark red blood came out of the hole – which is why they thought her witch's marks had been erased'. Nevertheless, Fontaine was at a loss to explain how or why this had happened and, while making one or two tentative suggestions, decided to leave the final word to those best fitted to deliver it – theologians.

What did such a mark look like? Descriptions vary considerably and authorities did not always agree with one another. A Scottish source describes it as 'sometimes like a blew spot, or a little tate [lump], or reid spots like flea biting' (J. Bell: *Tryall of Witchcraft*, 1705). The late sixteenth-century French advocate and judge Henri Boguet, on the other hand, tells us that the mark sometimes resembled an animal's footprint, such as a hare's foot, and that he himself had seen one almost as large as a coin, with several 'threads' extending from its centre to its circumference. 'The mark of Belcuenotte who was burned at Besançon was above her pudendum, a little lower than her navel, and stood out from the skin just like the fruit of a mallow-plant, or a chicken's or pigeon's arse. She herself stuck a large needle into it in our presence. The mark which Guillaume Proby d'Auchay found on the right side of her neck was the same size as a small coin and was brownish in colour' (*Discours des sorciers*, chapter 50). Louise Servant, nicknamed 'La Surgette', had on her left thigh a mark the size of a large nail-head; while the mark of Jean Del Vaulx, the monastic witch whose case was described by Del Rio, looked, we are told, like a small black dog.

This process of examining by piercing with a needle obviously involved methods which might be none too gentle. In 1624, not far from the French town of Vesoul in Haute-Saône, a woman was pierced so deeply that the surgeon could not retrieve his needle. But, to be fair, this was exceptional violence. Other surgeons seem to have approached their duties with less vigour and more objectivity. In 1635, for example, a peasant, Lazare Lamy, told the surgeon that the Devil had marked him just above his anus, next to the coccyx. 'I felt [the scar] and pricked it in six or seven places', the surgeon reported, 'both on the said scar and around it, without Lamy's complaining of any pain, even though the piercings were quite deep. However, they all drew blood' – a genuine witch's mark should not have done so – 'and the scar was of a colour similar to those caused by burns, wounds, and so forth. So one cannot say what originally caused it'. The honesty is worth remarking.

But a witch's mark, often likened to the mark of Cain or of the Beast, did not always take the form of a relatively small, insensitive spot. Extensive parts of the body could be rendered unfeeling by Satan. Del Rio, for example, was told by the Jesuit Provincial of the Spanish Netherlands that in 1599 a little witch-girl was arrested and subjected to savage whippings and scorching of her feet; yet she felt no pain at all until, on a priest's advice, an *Agnus Dei* (a disk of wax stamped with the image of Christ as a lamb) was hung round her neck, at which point awareness of pain began to return (*Disquisitiones Magicae* Book 2, question 21). On the other hand, a witch's distinguishing mark might not be on her flesh but in her eyes, as we saw from the case of Margaret Atkin. Boguet, too, noted that some witches recognised each other by some small blemish or spot in the eye, and that witches very often had a double pupil in one eye – a sign so noticeable as to be almost a deformity, one might think, and therefore visible to others besides a fellow-witch. Boguet also remarked that not every witch was marked by Satan and gave his opinion that the Devil left his mark only on those about whose loyalty he entertained some doubt, drawing a comparison between buyers whose word alone was good enough for a seller, and those the seller obliged to sign a written contract.

If such marks existed, clearly they could be found, but they generally needed an expert to probe for them and to announce authoritatively that a particular spot had been produced unnaturally by contact with a preternatural entity. The circumstances of pricking varied, of course, from case to case, locality to locality, and suspect to suspect, but one should probably discount the notion that most prickers spent hours investigating all the cicatrices they might come across on any given body. In a period when virtually everyone from knight to peasant and peasant's wife could well collect scars of all kinds during the course of their daily labours, it seems unlikely that a pricker would waste his time on marks which were self-evidently natural, especially as if he did, his conclusions and his reputation and further work which depended on them might well be called in question by the other officials present, who would be as acquainted with natural scars and blemishes as he.

Who, then, was a pricker? Doctors, as we have seen, were capable of turning their expertise to this diagnostic problem, while in France it was often the common executioner who acted as a *piqueur*, perhaps because it was thought his experience as a torturer would have taught him to be able to distinguish significant blemishes and scars from those present from birth or acquired through work or physical deprivation. But perhaps the most obvious people who were used in the capacity of testers were men who had, by dint of practice and an acquired history of apparent success, set themselves up in this trade and gained a local reputation in the art of pricking. One of the best-known of these is Matthew Hopkins who, together with his partner John Stearne, was responsible for a large number of identifications in East Anglia during the 1640s. But the art was actually cultivated more in Scotland which saw a large number of prickers at work, especially during the decade and a half between *c*.1648 and 1662.

For example, there was George Cathie, who was operating in Lanarkshire in November 1649. The presbytery, which had sent for him, was duly informed in December that 'upon the last day in November last bypast, in the tolbooth of Lanark, before famous [respectable] witnesses... and by consent of the forenamed suspected women of witchcraft... the said George did prik pinnes in everie one of them, and in diverse of them without paine the pinne was put in, as the witnesses can testifie'. Cathie's career, however, was soon to come to an end. On 10 April 1650 the presbytery of Haddington recorded that 'Janet Coutts [a confessing witch] declared judicially before the commissioners of her trial that the chief motive and principal enticer of her to delate innocent persons as guilty of witchcraft was George Cathie who, within three days of her first confession, entered in a bargain and contract with the deponer that she should delate many persons whom he might be put to try anent the witches' mark, and to profit thereby, and he would endeavour to get her life prolonged enough' (*CH2/185/6*). The presbytery cited him to appear before it. He failed to come throughout the rest of April but, probably because the civil magistrate to whom the ministers had applied to force him to comply had done his work, he did present himself on 1 May and denied any conspiracy with Janet. The presbytery, however, does not seem to have believed him, for it issued instructions to deal with the civil authorities and ask for his arrest.

But more notorious yet was John Kincaid whose name appears frequently in kirk and presbytery session records during this same period. The Kincaids originally came from Stirlingshire and seem to have had their fair share of black sheep; for the name surfaces in criminal records from time to time – in 1562, a William Kincaid was put on trial for rape; in 1565 James and Malcolm Kincaid were involved in an affray in Glasgow; closer to home, Margaret Kincaid from Campsie parish, whither the Kincaid family traced its roots, was accused of incest; and a Philip Kincaid was put on trial in Edinburgh for selling two men poison in 1658. John himself was a resident of Tranent, a small town about a mile south-east of Prestonpans and about 3.5 miles east of Musselburgh. William Kincaid, son of a John Kincaid, was christened there on 14 April 1635 and, if the two Johns are one and the same, it means that John had been living in Tranent for a good fourteen or fifteen years before evidence of his career as a pricker surfaces.

He had made himself known as a pricker some time before 1649, for in June that year we find him making a formal declaration before witnesses that he had been asked to prick certain suspect persons who were convened in the castle of Dirleton, a small town a few miles west of North Berwick.

The which day, in presence of [named officials], Patrick Watson in West Fenton and Menie Haliburton his spous, bruitted and long suspect of witchcraft, of thair own frie will uncompellit, hearing that I, John Kincaid underwritten, wes in the toune of Dirltoune and had some skill and dexterity in trying of the divillis marke in personis of such as wer suspect to be witches, came to the broad hall in the Castell of Dirltoune, and desyred me, the said John Kincaid, to use my tryall

of thame, as I had done on utheris; which, when I had done, I found
the divillis marke upon the bak syde of the said Patrik Watsone, a littill
under the point of his left shoulder, and upon the left syde of the said
Menie Halyburtoun hir neck, a littill above her left shoulder, whairof
thay wer not sensible after I had tryed the same as exactlie as ever I did
any uthers. This I testifie to be of veritie upon my credit and conscience.

(RPC 2nd series, 8.195)

Clearly by this time Kincaid had acquired some kind of reputation as a
pricker and must, therefore, have been at work in the area for a while.
It may seem extraordinary that the two suspects had actually asked
Kincaid to come and test them – their personal danger should his test
prove positive was very great – but it was by no means unknown for
accused persons, perhaps fully confident of their own innocence, perhaps putting on a display of bravado in the face of their growing
predicament, to invite a pricker to subject them to his pin. Indeed,
Kincaid was later fetched to Newbattle in July 1661 at the request of
Isobel Ferguson who wanted this chance to prove herself not guilty.

After the Dirleton incident, Kincaid seems to have remained in the
district, for on 8 August that year the presbytery of Haddington
employed him to prick seven women and one man and, having
obtained his testimony that these people had the mark, instructed the
local minister to have them tried before the kirk session. During the
kirk session of Stow on 2 September, Kincaid found the Devil's mark
on James Henrison and his wife, and it is recorded that Marion
Henrison was burned. (Marion may have been James's wife, but
Scottish women usually kept their own name after marriage, and so
Marion is more likely to have been James's sister or daughter.) On 9
September, Kincaid was in Corstorphine where he found two marks
on Marion Inglis, and on 18 December he pricked Bessie Masterton
in Dunfermline and was paid twenty merks for his trouble. The merk
was a silver coin worth about 1s 8d sterling [8.5 new pence] after
1603. Kincaid was therefore being paid just over £1 13s 0d sterling
[£1.65]. It is impossible to suggest a meaningful value for this in terms

of the present day, but some idea may be gauged by relating it to the price of a bap, a small thick roll of bread rather like a morning roll. Kincaid's fee would have enabled him to buy forty ten-penny [10d] baps, each weighing fourteen ounces, according to the regulation of oatbread by Stirling town council in 1638.

In May 1650 he was called to test a Katharine Smith, and five years later on 7 February he was summoned yet again to test a Katharine Smith (perhaps a different one, although it was not unknown for suspects to come before the authorities more than once) in the presence of Mr Walter Bruce, minister, Mr John Wemyss and John Douglas who recorded that they had seen him 'put a long pin in her body without sense or blood, which is called the Devil's mark'. Subsequent investigation took a long time, for it was not until 10 December that year that Katharine finally came to trial. On 13 June 1657 he was back home in Tranent after a visit to Linlithgow where he searched Agnes Robert, imprisoned on suspicion of witchcraft, and found a mark in the small of her back. His testimony thereto gives evidence he could not write, for it is signed by his initials (JC26/22/3/5). A week later he searched and pricked Janet Bruce in what the record refers to as the local prison-house (which may have meant a tolbooth but could have referred simply to an ordinary house which had a room or cellar usually employed as a temporary holding-place. The lock-up in Tranent as late as 1837, for example, consisted of a small room in the constable's house). He found four marks on her with a pin whose length is actually drawn in the recording document – it is 2⅛ inches long – and on 30th he signed, with his own mark, a declaration that these were diabolical in origin. Poor Janet Bruce attempted to commit suicide. 'William Forrester chirurgeon [surgeon] in Tranent doth declare that the foresaid Jonett Bruce had gottin poysone which causes greatt instimulatione and swelling in her body, and if that she had not vomit the same, which is known to be of truth, she had died' (JC26/22/3/1).

A document dated 28 August 1657 finds Kincaid at Dalkeith. 'The which day John Kinkaid, tryer of the witches marke, aftir in calling upon the name of the Lord by Mr Hugh Campbell, minister in

Dalkeith, gave his oath of fidelitie in tryeing of Catherine Cass, whether she had the witches mark or not; and after tryall the said John Kinkaide gave his great oath that he had found two witches marks and ane other upon hir shoulder; and in verificatione to the trueth of this, he hes annexed his marke hereunto before Sir James Richardson of Smeaton, Major Archibald Wathell, William Scott chamberlain [town bailie], and Mr Hugh Campbell, and I, John Symson, public notary' (JC26/22/5/6).

In 1659 he was back in Tranent. In March he found two marks on Christian Cranston, one in her right armpit, the other on her leg. On 6 April he searched Helen Simbeard and found three; on 23rd and 27th Janet Thomson was subjected to his ministrations, and on 27th Barbara Cochrane, who had two marks on the back of her neck towards the left shoulder. 'He did put in a long pin in each of them, whereof she was not sensible; and immediately thereafter, the said Barbara did cry out in presence of the justices of peace, "Foul thief, thou hast deceived me! Now, thou hast deceived me now!"' Whom did she mean? Was she reproaching Satan, the thief of her soul? Or was she accusing Kincaid himself, implying that he was taking money in return for false evidence? On 17 June, 'the bailie William Scott and the minister caused John Kincaid in Tranent, the ordinary pricker, search [Christian Wilson] for the mark, which he found to be in her left arm at the very first entering upon his search: which he averred to be the Devil's mark, for the pin passed quite through her arm, and she found not the least pain of it, neither knew she where the pin was put in; for when we asked her where she thought it was (because she said she was mightily tormented with it), she answered that it was upon her shoulder' (JC26/27/9/2).

It is difficult to interpret what was going on here. There are many points on the body which are insensible to pain (one has only to avoid nerve-endings), and so it is perfectly possible that many of those tested by Kincaid and the other prickers really did feel nothing when the pin entered certain places. But Christian seems either to have been trying to trick Kincaid by claiming she felt pain when in fact she did not, or genuinely to have felt the effect of the pin in a spot removed from the point of entry. The same situation can be seen on 17 June 1661 when Kincaid pricked Janet Paiston in Dalkeith. Kincaid found two marks (using pins about three inches long, we are told), but when Janet was asked where she thought the pins were put in, she pointed to another part of her body.

Kincaid's career finally ended in 1662. On 9 January, application was made to the Privy Council for his arrest because '[he] takes upon him at his oune hand without warrand or order to prick and try these persons who are suspect to be guilty of the abominable cryme of witchcraft'. Investigation followed, and a report to the Council on 1 April said that 'there hath bein great abuses committed by John Kincaid... whereby in all probabilitie many innocents have suffered'. So he was imprisoned in the tolbooth of Edinburgh from where, nine weeks later, he issued a petition for his release on caution (bail). The petitioner, the Justice-General and his deputes read, 'is now become so infirme and diseased of body, being ane old man, that if he be not speedilie putt to libertie, it will be to the great hazard of his lyfe'. The appeal lords granted his request under two conditions: first, his caution was posted at £1,000 Scots (something over £80 sterling), a very large sum of money; and secondly, he was to refrain from pricking or torturing any person suspected of witchcraft in future without a warrant from the Council or his Majesty's Justice deputes (*RPC* 3rd series, 1.132, 224).

These are interesting phrases. The reference to a warrant makes it clear that Kincaid had been arrested on the purely legal grounds that he had been operating without authorisation. Does this mean that the many other prickers had had some kind of licence? No written warrant appears to have survived among the records (which does not mean to say that such warrants did not exist, of course), but without some such written evidence of authority, how did local officials know that a pricker who presented himself or whom they summoned was not acting contrary to the law in what he did or was asked to do? Was the whole system of pricking unofficial, resting upon tacit trust and unspoken complicity? One's suspicion is strengthened by a report in the records of the Privy Council that, on 8 August 1662, the Lords heard a petition from John Hay, aged over sixty, who 'such hes bein the arrogancie and presumption of one Jon Dick, pricker, that, without any warrand from the Councill, to whom only the power and juris-diction of torture appertaineth, assumed to himself the power of pricking, and amongst others, some whereof he pricked to death, as is most nottour, did prick and shave the petitioner, thereby to bring a staine of perpetuall infamie and disgrace upon him' (*RPC* 3rd series, 1.251–2). Dick was duly arrested and imprisoned in the tolbooth of Edinburgh. Once again, there is a reference to lack of authorisation, so it looks as though the Privy Council had decided to clamp down on the activities of people who were undoubtedly responsible, as Hopkins had been in East Anglia, for exacerbating an unpleasant and dangerous situation, even if they had not actually created it. But the Lords' actions were rooted in their objection to Kincaid's and Dick's usurpation of Conciliar authority, not in any doubts they may suppos-edly have had about the validity of pricking itself.

The reference to torture is even more interesting because it is rather odd. 'Torture' had then, as it has now, a specific meaning in law. Article 1 of the 1984 United Nations Convention Against Torture, for exam-ple, defines torture as 'any act by which severe pain or suffering, whether physical or mental, is intentionally inflicted on a person for such purposes as obtaining from him or a third person information or a confession, punishing him for an act he has committed, or intimidat-ing or coercing him or a third person, or for any reason based on dis-crimination of any kind, when such pain or suffering is inflicted by or at the instigation of or with the consent or acquiescence of a public official or other person acting in an official capacity.' Certain aspects of this definition need to be changed for reference to medieval and early modern times, however, since it seems to have been assumed then that the infliction of pain would be carried out with the assistance of instruments, such as the rack, strappado or thumbscrews. The condi-tions endured by prisoners in prison would therefore have been classed as mal- or ill-treatment rather than torture.

So what did the Privy Council mean by its use of the term? There is no implication here that either Kincaid or Dick had set up a private torturing business similar to Richard Topcliffe's operations in England under Elizabeth Tudor. How, then, was it possible for Dick to prick some people to death, as the Council alleged? Are we to infer that they died of shock either during or soon after his ministrations? Or that they died from the harsh conditions of their imprisonment, which were then tacitly associated with or blamed upon the suspects' trial by pricking? Or that he pricked too carelessly or savagely and thereby severed an artery, which caused the accused to die? An earlier hearing before the Privy Council on 19 May explains the phraseology, in Hay's case at least:

> Such hath bein the unreasonable and boundlesse furie of some mali-
> tious enemies that they bryb ane cheating fellow, named John Dick, to
> fix ane blott of perpetuall infamie upon the petitioner by shaving all
> the parts of his body, and therafter pricking him to the great effusion
> of his blood and with much torture to his body, all which as it was
> done without commission.
>
> (*RPC* 3rd series, 1.210)

Here, then, we have an insight into this particular incident. This was no ordinary pricking, but an attempt to inflict as much shame and pain upon John Hay as could be managed under cover of witch-investigating. The episode illustrates well the relative ease with which people might lay claim to this activity and exploit it for a variety of purposes which had nothing to do with witchcraft. It also offers a warning about the appearance of the word 'torture' in the records. It is here a synonym for 'pain', and its conjunction with a reference to Dick's lack of authority is meant to remind the reader, as it would have been a matter of some concern to the Lords of Council themselves, that the prerogative of inflicting *judicial* torture (i.e., 'torture' in the proper sense of the word), had been wrested from them by this unofficial fellow in the pursuit of a private vendetta by some third parties not named in the record.

Several such prickers came before the Council, which stopped them in their tracks. They included, as we have seen, Kincaid himself;

but oddly enough, if Kincaid fell victim to the Privy Council's desire to put an end to illegal activities during the investigation of witches, it may have been because of an earlier body, the Committee of Estates, that he embarked on his career as a pricker in the first place. The Committee, which had been instituted as an organ of Scottish government in June 1640, issued commissions for 157 witch-trials, a rather large number, in the second half of 1649. So it may be no coincidence that Kincaid appears to have emerged as a pricker of witches at about that same time, although documentation of an earlier period may simply not have survived, of course.

Some Scottish prickers certainly turned their trade into a business, as can be seen from a detailed account of a pricking across the border in Newcastle in 1649 or 1650. The local magistrates had decided to purge the town of its witches and sent for a Scottish pricker to 'try such who should be brought to him, and to have twenty shillings a peece, for all he could condemn as witches, and free passage thither and back again'. This arrangement was an open invitation to fraud, of course, and we cannot be surprised to find that the man was later arrested and hanged in Scotland, confessing at the gallows that he had been the cause of the death of more than 220 women in both Scotland and England for the gain of twenty shillings each. The account of his activities in Newcastle and Northumberland is chilling:

> When the Sergeants had brought the said witch-finder on horse-back to town, the magistrates sent their bell-man through the town, ringing his bell, and crying, all people that would bring any complaint against any woman for a witch, they should be sent for, and tryed by the person appointed.
>
> Thirty women were brought into the town-hall, and stript, and then openly had pins thrust into their bodies, and most of them was found guilty, near twenty-seven of them by him, and set aside.
>
> The said reputed witch-finder acquainted lieut. Colonel Hobson, that he knew women, whether they were witches or no, by their looks, and when the said person was searching of a personable, and good-like woman, the said colonel replyed and said, surely this

woman is none, and need not be tryed, but the scotch-man said she was, for the town said she was, and therefore he would try her; and presently in sight of all the people, laid her body naked to the waste, with her cloathes over her head, by which fright and shame, all her blood contracted in one part of her body, and then he ran a pin into her thigh, and then suddenly let her coats fall, and then demanded whether she had nothing of his in her body, but did not bleed, but she being amazed, replied little, then he put his hand up her coats, and pulled out the pin, and set her aside as a guilty person, and the child of the devil, and fell to try others whom he made guilty.

Lieutenant colonel Hobson, perceiving the alteration of the foresaid woman, by her blood settling down in her right parts, caused that woman to be brought again, and her cloaths to be pulled up to her thigh, and required the Scot to run a pin into the same place, and then it gushed out of blood, and the said Scot cleared her, and said, she was not a child of the devil.

So soon as he had done, and received his wages, he went into Northumberland, to try women there, where he got some, three pound a peece, but Henry Ogle Esq., a late member of parliament, laid hold on him, and required bond of him, to answer the sessions, but he got away for Scotland, and it was conceived if he had stayed, he would have made most of the women of the north witches, for money'.[5]

Like this anonymous tryer and the Englishman Hopkins, then, Kincaid and his fellow prickers can be said to have contributed in no small measure to a major outbreak of witch-prosecutions; but one needs to ask whether it is at all possible that he or any of the others undertook their specialised work because they were aware of possessing a special gift which enabled them to recognise a witch, or whether they were all just exploiting a situation which had arisen without them but which they exacerbated in their diligence to turn other people's misfortunes into cash.

George Cathie, as we have seen, was undoubtedly guilty of false practice, as he had colluded with a woman to make untrue accusations, and Kincaid himself was accused of committing great abuses to the harm of many innocents. Nevertheless, one is obliged to introduce, yet again, a note of caution into one's view of what seems to be a straightforward matter. If pricking a person in order to discover insensitive spots on the body was not a skilled business, why did the authorities bother to send for and use prickers at some expense to the public funds? Why not simply take a pin and test the accused themselves? Moreover, if pricking was a matter of piercing until an insensitive place was found, why would not the authorities have regarded any prolonged efforts by the pricker merely as signs of his incompetence or charlatanry? As we have seen from the Newcastle episode, people were certainly aware that fraud was possible, and were willing to try to expose it. It was surely essential to the successful pricker that he demonstrate his particular ability by discovering the mark or marks fairly quickly. (Again, the Newcastle prickings seem to have taken little time to produce their results.) If he could do this and, laying aside for the moment the presence of fraud, one remembers the testimony of witnesses of Kincaid's activities, the pricker's ability to find a mark which would not cause pain, or bleed, argues a degree of skill, so that one finds oneself asking how the pricker acquired his skill, since amateur brodding in the early stages of his attempted career would have been unlikely to give him the kind of reputation he needed to turn professional.

It is not sufficient to declare, as Christina Larner did, that prickers 'understood the principle of confused sensation and which parts of the body could be most successfully assaulted. They may have had knowledge of the points used by acupuncturists',[6] since such a declaration does not explain how the pricker came by such specialised knowledge. Indeed, the Privy Council itself did not know, for on 16 February 1632 it arranged for investigation to be made into the pricker John Balfour who 'has taken upon him the knowledge to discover persouns guiltie of the cryme of witchecraft by remarking the devills marke upon some part of thair persouns and bodeis... and upon the presumptioun of this his knowledge goes athort the countrie abusing simple and ignorant people for his private gayne and commoditie'. He was to appear in person before the Lords of Council 'to answere such things as sall be demanded of his tuicheing his knowledge on the discoverie of the cryme aforesaid, and how and by what meanes he hes the same'. Balfour came on 23rd and explained that the first time he pricked was at the request of the minister of Tranent – Kincaid's home town; one wonders whether the two men knew each other and whether Kincaid learned his skill from Balfour. The Lords heard him out and decided 'his knowledge in this mater hes onelie beene conjecturall' (that is, had been personal opinion based on insufficient evidence), 'and most unlawfullie used within Gods kirk'. So they forbade him to continue (*RPC* 2nd series, 4.427, 433). But their investigations into *how* he had acquired his knowledge seem either to have been fruitless or not to have been recorded.

If pricking was one flawed means of detecting a witch, swimming was another. Swimming was not a practice used in Scotland but it was common elsewhere, especially in Germany. The process was succinctly described by Johann Godelmann.

Women who have become suspect as workers of poisonous magic [*veneficae*] through reputation or confession are arrested and immediately subjected to further questioning by a number of ignorant German judges. The arrested women are brought beyond the city and, with their right hand bound to their left foot and their left hand to their right foot, are thrown into cold water. It is believed that if they float, they are witches [*veneficae*], but if they sink, they are innocent.

(*De magis, veneficis, et lamiis* [1610], Book 3, chapter 5)

The origins of this probation go back well beyond the ordeals commonly used in the Middle Ages to test a person's innocence – trial by combat, holding and carrying a red-hot object for a certain length of time, and so forth. Testing a magical practitioner by cold water can be found among the laws of ancient Babylonia, and it may be possible to trace its subsequent passage via the Scythians into the regular customs of the Eastern Slavic world. Certainly it was well established there by the twelfth century and migrated thence to western Russia where it continued in use far into the nineteenth century, the last recorded instance coming from the Ukraine in 1885. Its heyday in Western Europe came in the late sixteenth and seventeenth centuries. Usually employed by crowds or large groups of people in a heightened emotional state, such swimmings could quickly turn very violent, and in some instances the accused person was simply lynched. Swimming was a very public test, as opposed to the search for marks, which was conducted in comparative private, and the manner in which the suspect was prepared and treated could easily pre-determine the outcome. In May 1594, for example, several people were arrested in Bar-sur-Seine and subjected to this probation in the presence of their entire villages, one man being thrown into the water with a fifty-pound weight attached to his body. But even without this kind of extremity, the suspect might well die from drowning or from the cold. Such, at any rate, was the experience of France where, strictly speaking, probation by cold water should have taken place only after sentence had been passed in a court of law, and so often did not.

In England, the method of securing the witch to be tested was subject to variations and, at least on occasion, no less chicanery. A pamphlet published in 1613 gives details about the swimming of Mary Sutton and her mother. They were accused by one Master Enger of causing deaths among his horses and pigs, and of various other calamities; and after a period in which his woes multiplied, as he perceived, at the hands of these women, he happened to fall in conversation with a friend of his from the north of England.

> Upon Master Enger's relation of what had happened, the gentleman demanded if he had none in suspicion that should do these wrongs unto him. 'Yes', quoth Master Enger, and therewithal he named this Mary Sutton and her mother, and told him the particulars of his losses and miseries. His friend understanding this, advised him to take them, or any one of them, to his mill dam (having first shut up the mill gates that the water might be at highest) and then, binding their arms cross, stripping them into their smocks and leaving their legs at liberty, throw them into the water.

Yet lest they should not be witches, and that their lives might not be in danger of drowning, let there be a rope tied about their middles, so long that it may reach from one side of your dam to the other, where on each side let one of your men stand, that if she chance to sink they may draw her up and preserve her. Then, if she swim, take her up and cause some women to search her, upon which, if they find any extraordinary marks about her, let her the second time be bound, and have her right thumb bound to her left toe and her left thumb to her right toe, and your men with the same rope (if need be) to preserve her, and be thrown into the water when, if she swim, you may build upon it that she is a witch. I have seen it often tried in the north country.

The morrow after, Master Enger rode into the fields where Mary Sutton [the daughter] was, having some of his men to accompany him; where after some questions made unto her, they assayed to bind her on horseback when, all his men being presently stricken lame, Master Enger himself began to remember that, once rating her about his man, he was on the sudden in the like perplexity; and then, taking courage and desiring God to be his assistance, with a cudgel which he had in his hand he beat her till she was scarce able to stir.

At which his men presently recovered, bound her to their master's horse, and brought her home to his house; and shutting up his mill gates, did as before the gentleman had advised him. When being thrown in the first time, she sunk some two foot into the water with a fall, but rose again and floated upon the water like a plank. Then he commanded her to be taken out, and had women ready that searched her and found under her left thigh a kind of teat which, after, the bastard son confessed her spirits in several shapes – as cats, moles, etc. – used to suck her.

Then was she the second time bound cross her thumbs and toes, according to the former direction, and then she sunk not at all but sitting upon the water, turned round about like a wheel, or as that which commonly we call a whirlpool; notwithstanding Master Enger's men standing on each side of the dam with a rope tossing her up and down to make her sink, but could not.

The prevalence of such determined efforts to prove the suspect a witch certainly helped to sow doubts in the minds of writers on witchcraft about the validity of the practice. In theory it should have worked. The German physician Wilhelm Scribonius wrote a treatise, *A Letter concerning the Examination and Purgation of Witches* [sagae] *by Cold Water* (1583), in which he argued that there is a natural antipathy between witches and water, which causes the water to reject them, and that the reason witches float is because Satan is by nature very light and has more in common with air than with water, so that during swimming he either supports the witches and raises them on his back, or pours himself into their whole body and thus lightens it by occupying it. Another reason, he said, was that God knows who is guilty and who is not, and endows the body of a witch with a peculiar and specific lightness, thereby causing her or him to float and so reveal his or her true nature.

Generally speaking, however, scholars were hostile to his arguments and attacked him vigorously in print. Johann Wier observed that the natural reason anyone floated was exactly the same whether he or she was innocent or guilty, but that if the reason were preternatural, it was because the Devil was making the person float in order to hoax the magistrate (*De praestigiis daemonum* Book 6, chapter 9). It is an interesting parallel to De Lancre's proposition about the falsity of appearances. On the one hand the suspect really is floating and in theory is therefore a witch; but actually he or she would sink were it not for the unseen effort of the Devil, which is keeping her or him afloat. It is one of Scribonius's explanations given a particular slant. Del Rio, on the other hand, while recording that in his day probation by swimming was common throughout Germany, especially the area round Westphalia, roundly dismisses Scribonius's appeal to both God's and Satan's ability to make witches float. In essence, he agrees both God and Satan *could* produce this phenomenon, but denies that they actually do, since there exists no good proof (he says) that either has wished to do so (*Disquisitiones Magicae* Book 4, question 5). Johann Godelmann also objected and offered his own eye-witness account of an incident to show that the proof could be seriously flawed:

In the year 1588, while I was going from Borussia to Livonia, a very rich noble invited me to his castle. Here a worker of poisonous magic [*venefica*] had been condemned to be burned the following day because of the enormous crimes she had committed by her magical and devilish art. I asked if she had first been thrown into water, according to the usual practice, to test whether she was guilty. He said no, and I advised him to try it (because I wanted to find out, by this method, if this test by cold water was valid or not). But after the witch [*venefica*], with her limbs bound, had been thrown into cold water by the executioner, she sank immediately. The nobleman wrote to me later that he tried the same thing with six captive witches [*veneficae*], but they had all sunk; and at the end of his letter he wrote, 'Now at last I believe you, that this sign is false, diabolical, and mad, and can deceive an unwary magistrate'.

(*De magis, veneficis, et lamiis* Book 3, chapter 5)

Johann Fickler, a Catholic priest, arguing before the University of Ingolstadt in 1592, had no time for ordeals of any kind as a demonstration of someone's guilt. 'Those who are subjected to probation by the torture of cold or boiling water or red-hot iron, and confess to an act of harmful magic [*maleficium*], and their confession has not been elicited during the course of any preceding legal hearing: because such a proof is inimical to natural law and to reason... they cannot in any way be found guilty' (*Disputatio juridica de maleficis et sagis*, proposition 123). The Bishop of Trier, Peter Binsfeld, went even further in his condemnation. Having discussed the matter in detail, he offered three conclusions: (1) anyone who was active in carrying out this probation was guilty of a mortal sin; (2) so too were those who believed in its efficacy unless they could show they were ignorant individuals; and (3) the confession of anyone subjected to swimming and then tortured as a result of the test, and who admitted to being a witch, was worthless and invalid (*Tractatus de confessionibus maleficorum et sagarum*, 1579).

Catholic and Protestant demonologists thus combined to dismiss swimming as both useless and illegal. Their opinions, however, had little or no effect on the vast, less learned majority, since most people did not or could not read them; and in consequence, swimming remained part of the popular repertoire in several places in Europe for detecting who was a witch and who was not. We need to be slightly careful, however, before we draw the easy conclusion that this dichotomy represents a cultural gap between the more civilised, sceptical scholar and the reactionary, hysterical crowd. The principal objections scholars had to the process were that it was illegal and untrustworthy. Their reservations had nothing to do with their acceptance of the reality of witches – that they shared with the rest of their communities. But their reservations had the tacit effect of indicating that the scholars were people apart from the unlettered multitude and superior to it. Consequently, it was in scholars' personal interests to express qualified doubts about a process frequently used by their intellectual inferiors, because that expression flattered their sense of self-worth and reinforced their belief that they were morally superior to others.

On the other hand, the same kind of observation can be made of 'the crowd'. If witches are identifiable and procedures for identification exist, once identified these people are exposed as representatives and agents of 'The Other', and their testers thereby confirmed in their collective identities as 'The Righteous'. Swimming a suspect witch, therefore, was an attractive way of publicly demonstrating to one's friends and neighbours a fellowship in right thinking and right behaviour, and a community in opposition to 'otherness' which, as everyone knew, hovered constantly in the background and every so often threatened to bring chaos and ruin to settled society.

6

ELIZABETH JAMESON:
IMPLICATING ONE'S NEIGHBOURS

Identifying a witch, as we have seen, could be and was done in a variety of ways and might involve the expert knowledge of several different professions, each of which had, over a period of time, accumulated a great deal of experience both in the application and the development of theory based upon observation. When it came to the interrogation and any subsequent trial of a witch, these various expertises came into play as one party endeavoured to conduct a dialogue with the other, each having certain fundamentals in common: the reality of God, of Satan and the demonic world; the effectiveness of certain acts of magic; and the substantiality of magical intention which led to those acts or the request that they be performed. It is too easily forgotten in the facile rush to suggest that one side oppressed the other and that confessions of guilt represent little more than fantasy produced by pain or fear or exhaustion, that in a culture in which all classes accepted the reality of magic and its eventualities – with varying degrees of reservation on various points, but accepted by and large nevertheless – many of those accused of working acts of magic were guilty and their confessions, whether produced voluntarily or under duress, were genuine either in whole or in part, depending on the details of each charge. The notion that all magical operations, from the trivial and harmless cure to the dangerous and malevolent death-wish, were no more than the products of hallucination or a terrified wish to appease authorities who were themselves labouring under some kind of class-based delusion, is to make nonsense of history and to trivialise our forebears. It may be difficult for modern Westerners to accept that earlier periods genuinely looked at the world from a quite different viewpoint which was both intellectually sophisticated and grounded in experienced observation, but the effort needs to be made. However uncomfortable we may find it, many accusations and confessions of witchcraft may well have been true or have contained enough truth to render a 'guilty' verdict both just and justifiable. If someone believes in the reality of witchcraft and performs, with belief and intention, magical operations her contemporaries call 'witchcraft', then she is a witch; if she is later accused of performing those acts and confesses to have performed them, her confession is genuine; and if those actions contravene a national or local statute which forbids them under pain of stated penalties, a verdict of guilty is only to be expected. 'Delusion' does not come into it.

Now, in the majority of trials for witchcraft we can detect three possible levels of social interaction, producing the dialogue I mentioned. One was the learned stratum, the inquisitors, the clergy, the doctors and the lawyers, who were at least acquainted with and usually deeply knowledgeable in the treatises, monographs and commentaries on all aspects of demonology, which had been written by their intellectual peers and superiors for their better information and instruction. Such literature is by no means uniform either in its propositions or in its conclusions, and therefore anyone who read it widely would find himself engaged, not in a constant and tedious repetition of the same tired premises regurgitated over and over again, but in a lively intellectual debate which touched upon almost every frontier of contemporary speculation and set up a constant challenge to the heady assumptions and explorations of what would now be called the natural sciences. Far from being retrogressive or petrifying, demonological studies were as much a part of the intellectual thrust of the early modern period as, for example, were contemporary developments in mathematics or astronomy. At this level, of course, the suspect or accused witch was marginally involved inasmuch as she or he was unlikely to be someone who even knew about the intricacies of these rarefied debates. But the lawyers, the clergy or the doctors involved might have at least some inkling of learned opinion and thus be inclined, if only subconsciously, to conduct their case and present their evidence in accordance with what they had read or what they considered to be the most verifiable interpretation of the facts before them – rather like forensic scientists and other expert witnesses in a modern murder trial.

Secondly, however, we have the non-expert official – the judge, the magistrate, the local clergyman – whose opinions were guided not so much by erudite demonological discussion as by practical experience and the social, economic, political or religious circumstances immediately obtaining in his neighbourhood. These people were acting under pressure, sometimes intense; for one of the points which has emerged from recent research is the extent to which trials for witchcraft were driven, not by learned theories, patriarchal conspiracies against women, or official attempts to regulate society (some of the older attempts to account for widespread prosecutions), but by local demand, often irresistible, to solve what was perceived as an immediate and local problem.

This brings us to the third level of engagement, which involves the neighbours, family and clients of the witch herself. Many accusers, many witnesses in these cases, as well as many of the accused, were women. The reasons for this are complex, but they point to an aspect of the trials, their causes and preliminary procedures, which has sometimes been subordinated to the notion that these cases illustrate a battle by men to keep women in subjection, the female accused being victims of a male-dominated legal and social system. But the extent to which accusations of being a witch arise from hostile dialogue between women means that witch-trials may be seen, at least in part (because this does not explain the phenomenon of male witches), as a continuation of inter-female struggle for power and status within a local community, using the male-dominated law as the ultimate weapon in that struggle. In as far as those trials may be interpreted as continuing dialogues started between disparate groups within a local community, they may also be seen as the acting-out of scripts very often devised and to a large extent co-written by women, regardless of how major were the parts played by men once those scripts ended up on the public stage.

How did these scripts begin? Not always in the same way, of course, but frequently with a quarrel. People in early modern Scotland (to choose one country by way of illustration), had a vivid way with words when it came to insulting each other. In 1670, for example, the kirk session of Anstruther Easter heard that Janet Moneypenny had called Isobel Anderson a whore and a dromedary who had bewitched her mother-in-law, in answer to which Isobel called Janet a thief and a randy-ridden witch. This angry exchange encapsulates the most common epithets employed by one angry person (usually a woman), against another (usually another woman), which one reads in the kirk and presbytery session records of the period – whore, thief, witch. Now, the business of being rude to an adversary cannot be altogether a matter of random insult and certainly was not so during the early modern period. There is no point in calling someone a whore if there is no fornication in the community, just as there is no point in calling someone a thief if the community knows no stealing; and indeed there would have been no sense in Janet Moneypenny's calling Isobel Anderson a dromedary had there not been something obvious about Isobel's appearance which made the epithet immediately meaningful and hurtful. Thus, we can legitimately infer that Isobel may have been a hunch-back.

Likewise, there is no point in calling somebody a witch unless the practice of witchcraft is known and accepted by the community as a feature of everyday life, no more exotic than theft or harlotry. The early modern period understood this point perfectly. In 1658, for example, it was recorded that 'Elspeth Scot called Agnes Paterson a quean [prostitute], and she said that if she had not been a quean she would not have called her one'.[7] We may also add that there is no point in calling someone a thief, a harlot or a witch if she is well known to be of blameless life. The accusations work only if she is a woman capable, like most other people, of sinning and falling from grace, and is known to have done so. What is more, the epithet becomes most effective if the person accused is known, or at least strongly suspected, to have committed the particular crime of which she is slandered. Something in the accused person's past or present behaviour may have directed her accuser to aim a well-chosen slur upon her character. Thus, in May 1676, a witness before the kirk session of St Monance testified that she heard Jean Watson say to Elspeth Morrison, 'Everybody says you are a witch [and] I tell you the plain verity – you are one! For you whimmled my Lord's boat' (a reference to the fact that a boat had overturned in the harbour); to which Jean added the sardonic observation that Elspeth must have had hot feet from the violent stamping to make it capsize.

A woman's reputation was her power-base. Strike at that, and she was undone, either for the time being or permanently. It is notable that accusations of theft, harlotry or witchcraft all call her honesty in question. It is often said that women were deeply affected by the standards of moral behaviour suggested to or imposed upon them by men, and there is obviously much truth in this. It is also true that they accepted these standards (whether willingly or perforce is another question, but the answer will vary from individual to individual and from time and place to time and place), and therefore that their mutual accusations of misconduct represent, among other things, attempts to maintain and uphold these same standards. But we may also note that women were intimately involved in the economy of their community, and so it was in their interests, as well as the interests of their menfolk, to be able to trust one another. Small communities are close-knit and inter-dependent. A thief does damage to those bonds; sex beyond or without marriage upsets them; malevolent magic threatens to destroy them. Moreover, these bonds bind everyone. Damage to one set may cast doubt, suspicion or unease over all the others. The modern anthropologist Jeanne Favret-Saada who investigated witchcraft in Normandy during the 1950s came to an interesting conclusion which rings true of the earlier period. Everyone is involved, one way or another. You are either a witch yourself, or someone who has been bewitched, or someone who can lift the bewitchment. No one is neutral. Everyone is caught somehow in the web of magic.

Name-calling was thus important. It involved an exchange which did damage to a woman's reputation, helped to establish or emphasise the negative side of her status and character in the community's perception of her, and made everyone uneasy about the strength of the bonds which were supposed to hold them all together. Name-calling, however, might often involve more than just a simple insult. Potentially serious charges might well be made, too. Take, for example, the case of Katharine Key. On 4 September 1653, Katharine was cited to appear before the kirk session of Newburgh for cursing the minister because he had barred her from communion. Now, cursing was not a straightforward matter. It was an act of verbal violence ritually expressed. Thus, in Anstruther Wester, Isobel Greson complained that Alison Ferny had 'sat doun on her knees and prayed that God would send a black day upon the said Isobel and her son'; while in Newburgh, Margaret Blyth was alleged to have said, 'Lord, let Henry Arnot never thrive, nor further gang [go], nor the goods that go before him, nor nothing he takes in hand', to which the witness added 'that she cam in among a pack of devils'. 'Sitting upon one's knees' is a ritual act. It is what one does in prayer. It was also the required form for expressing one's repentance for sin in front of a kirk session or congregation. Kneeling to curse, therefore, added a ritual dimension to the malison, which it was not difficult to interpret as humbling oneself before Satan in a parody of Christian abasement before God – and Katharine Key, we are told, had cursed the minister on her knees in the open street.

The minister replied by explaining to the session his reasons for banning Katharine from communion. There were five: (1) when someone in David Orme's house refused to give her milk, his cow produced nothing but blood until Katharine was sent for and cured it by slapping it on the side and saying, 'The cow will be well'; (2) much the same happened to John Philp who nearly lost a new-born calf until Katharine came and apparently cured it; (3) Katharine had been employed by the minister and his wife as a wet-nurse for their child, and when they decided to dismiss her and hand over the child's nursing to someone else, the child refused to suckle. Nor would it take milk again until it was brought back to Katharine; (4) when the time came for the child to be weaned, Katharine came to see it and took it in her arms, but thereafter, the session was told, the child girned and cried day and night until it died; and finally, (5) 'she is ane evil [woman], brute and fame, and so wes her mother before her' – in other words, she was a woman with the reputation of being a magical operator, and her mother had been known likewise in the community. This, and the information that Katharine was sent for to cure sick cows, suggests that Katharine, and perhaps her mother also, were thought to have specific powers or to be in possession of certain curative formulae, and were consulted by the inhabitants of Newburgh whenever a situation arose which her clients believed fell within her particular purview.

Was the minister taking revenge on Katharine for the death of his child by fetching her for trial in front of the session? I think not. His original action had simply been to ban her from taking communion. It was Katharine herself who had made things worse by cursing the minister in public. He was surely bound to do something about that. The charges against her involve two types of magical skill: *maleficium*, an act of hostile magic intended to bring hurt or even death to an animal or human being; and lifting a bewitchment – in three of the cases, a bewitchment Katharine herself was said to have laid already. Each time the injured party knew (or, if you like, believed), that Katharine was responsible and so sent for her to restore the magical balance in their favour. Notice, therefore, that Katharine was capable of exercising magic for both good and ill according to her personal decision, and that her community accepted the situation and used her as appropriate.

In the fourth charge, however, no such balance was achieved. Katharine, we are told, came to see the minister's child, who was healthy at the time of her visit, but who declined thereafter until finally it died. The clear implication is that Katharine killed her by magic, a negative aspect of her abilities emphasised (as one might expect in the circumstances of the kirk-investigation), by the assertion that she was a woman of evil reputation, like her mother. Why, then, one may ask had the minister and his wife employed her as their wet-nurse in the first place? The answer must lie in the local knowledge which has not been recorded: those multifarious details of everyday social intercourse which colour personal relations and combine, especially over a long period of time, to form a community's judgement of its separate members. The inhabitants of Newburgh knew Katharine infinitely better than we either do or can, and both the minister who employed her and the elders who heard his complaint against her were better able than we are to assess what she was really like. But the lacuna in our knowledge is a reminder that the recorded 'dialogue' between accused and examiners in these affairs often represents little more than a summary of a great range of complexities, and comes at the end of what was probably a series of conversations and exchanges whose exact words are usually lost in the official résumé, along with the tones of voice, verbal emphases, omissions, suggestions, misunderstandings, and the emotional gamut of responses to one another, which all parties involved displayed during the course of the investigative process.

The kirk session was scrupulously fair to Katharine during its inquiry into her case. For various reasons, however, the process dragged on for months, until March 1654, when it was referred to the presbytery where it continued to linger for over a year. (There is nothing sinister about this. Simple inefficiency explains it, and Katharine does not seem to have been imprisoned or subjected to any restraint on her movements while this was going on.) Finally, the ministers of the presbytery referred her case back to Newburgh, requiring the local minister to ask from the pulpit if anyone else in the community had any complaints of witchcraft to lay against her. This he did on 10 June 1655, but no one came forward, even though twelve people had testified to the truth of the minister's charges in September 1653. Clearly her 'evil' reputation was either not as great as had first been alleged, or the adverse stir to which she had given rise had dissipated during the intervening eighteen months. Whatever the reason for her neighbours' silence, the protracted affair was over.

Katharine apologised publicly to the minister at the end of the month, and her case was finally closed.

Accusations of killing a child by magic, then, were not necessarily enough to bring a suspect witch in front of a criminal court. Notice, too, that the Devil was not involved. There was no Sabbat, no flying through the air, no searching or pricking for witch's marks, no torture, no test by swimming, no old, half-witted woman living on the margins of her community. Katharine was employed as a wet-nurse. This probably means she was no older than her early thirties. The late medieval physician Giovanni Michele Savonarola, for example, recommended that a wet-nurse be aged between thirty-two and thirty-five because although younger women's milk was more plentiful, it was somewhat watery and therefore a more mature woman was to be preferred. Wet-nursing was also a position of high responsibility, for the common belief of the time was that a child not only imbibed physical qualities from his nurse's milk, but moral characteristics, too. The minister and his wife could surely not have been short of candidates for the post of wet-nurse to their daughter. So their deliberate choice of Katharine, in spite of her reputation as a healer of sick cows (a reputation which would have been based on her magical abilities, not on some anachronistic appreciation of any veterinary skills she may have had), seems to suggest that the mere existence and activity of a magical operator within a community subject to constant close moral investigation by the Church which, officially at least, was hostile to magic and 'superstitious' practices, were not necessarily sufficient to lead to prosecution. It is worth adding, too, that the charges brought against Katharine and the circumstances of her investigation are actually typical of the experience of suspect witches not only in Scotland but elsewhere in Europe as well, except in certain places at certain times under certain circumstances which produced both individual cases and bursts of group-prosecution highly vivid in their detail and appalling in their outcome, which have had a tendency to dominate popular imagination.

Still, if many, indeed most, cases died at the stage of the kirk session, some did make their way to the presbytery and could be recommended thence, at the presbyters' discretion, to the secular magistrates. Allan Guthrie from Largo was accused of using a charm at the marriage of James and Christian Black in October 1700. He had endeavoured to induce impotence in the groom by tying knots in some threads, a magical operation the session considered 'a matter of the greatest importance', for they referred him to the presbytery of St Andrews where his case was held under consideration until the following February. The presbytery then heard that Allan had been rebuked by the minister of Largo and adjudged this to be sufficient in consideration of Allan's age: he was only thirteen. Had he been older, he might well have suffered the fate of William Crichton from Dunfermline. An entry in the kirk session records for 6 August 1648 tells us: 'The quhilk day William Crichtoun compeirand, and being posed upon the delations [charges] given in against him, he denyit all. He was remitted to the magistrat to be imprisoned, which was done; and some few days thereaftir, being straitlie posed and dealt with be the minister and watchers, he came to a confession of sindrie things, and that he had made paction with the Devil to be his servand 24 yeirs and more since'. A note was later added to the record: 'Some few days thereftir he was burnt'. He was not burned alive: not in Scotland. The usual sentence for witchcraft there consisted of garrotting followed by burning of the dead body and escheatment of the dead person's moveable goods.

Such was the possible fate awaiting Elizabeth Jameson from Bo'ness, a seaport about three miles north of Linlithgow, who was put on trial towards the end of September 1624 in the High Court of Justiciary in Edinburgh on fifteen charges of witchcraft. The method of her 'discovery' was a common one, for she had been denounced the previous March or April by Jean Lilburne, a confessing witch who was tried and executed before Elizabeth's trial began. Jean had confessed to dancing round a post on the sea-shore at midnight, with the Devil leading the dance and others beside herself taking part. They were, she said, 'but the beggarly rank' except for one who was 'of the honester sort'. At first Jean professed herself unwilling to name names, 'fearing [as she said] that harm might come to her poor bairns', but was prevailed upon at last, partly by promises of Heaven and threats of Hell, partly by the sting of her own conscience, to name four of her companions, one of whom – 'she that was next to the Devill' – was Elizabeth (otherwise called Elspeth) Jameson, at whose particular desire the Devil filled a cockle-shell with water and then upset it in order to wreck a ship which was then at sea.

Jean also accused Katharine Blair who, upon being arrested and questioned, at first tried to brazen it out and indignantly denied that Elizabeth was a witch; but then in the face of Jean's sticking to her story, modified her denial and said that when Jean had taken her to see the dancers, 'I thought they had been fairy folk, and you told me that you knew some of them, but never one of them I knew'. Her interrogators then pressed her further about Elizabeth Jameson, to which Katharine replied, 'Faith, I will warrant you she is a greater witch than any of us and has been longer in the Devil's service'. A second, separate interrogation, however, saw her back-tracking. 'Sche fearid to speik of Elspet Jemiesoune albeit they socht to remove all occasioun of feare... [and] still sche denyit that ever sche knew hir in the devills companey, only hard this and that'. Pressed for details, Katharine admitted she had seen seven women at the dancing, but could not name any of them; and so she continued, evasive in spite of renewed questioning both in prison and on her way to execution, and 'the juges, seing hir so wavering and fearfull, gave no trust to hir depositione'.

The omissions which produced this official record are, to some extent, obvious and we can see clear jumps in her separate testimonies: (a) Elizabeth is not a witch; (b) I saw the dancers. I assumed they were fairies. I did not recognise anyone; (c) Elizabeth is a greater witch than the rest of us; (d) I am frightened to speak of Elizabeth. I saw nothing. I am only repeating what others told me; (e) I saw seven women. I do not know who they were. Now, it is often assumed that testimony from those accused of witchcraft was obtained by means of torture, browbeating, sleep deprivation, interrogatory deviousness, or a combination of any or all of these. Nevertheless, it is an assumption which, however consonant with modern sensibilities and apparently agreeable with evidence from various times and places, should not be made without great care in any individual case. Take the women's alleged dancing at midnight, for example. It is common to find suspect witches accused of meeting late at night or in the very early hours of the morning, and while this may be explained by reference to the pivotal place held by midnight in the hours of darkness – half-way through the night-period which was reckoned from six in the evening until six in the morning – we should also be aware that sleep patterns in the early modern period were not the same as ours. There is plenty of evidence from the sixteenth and seventeenth centuries that sleep was often segmented, experienced as two major intervals of sleep broken by an hour or more of wakefulness. Waking in the middle of the night was common, and people were not necessarily content to lie in bed until they slept again. For the poor and criminally-inclined, it was an ideal opportunity for thieving or murder under cover of darkness; while for the rest, it often provided occasion to visit neighbours and friends. Seeing people one knew up and about at midnight, therefore, was not necessarily a fiction the accused witch made up for the minister or magistrate. 'Midnight', of course, should not be taken in our literal sense. In an age when few people had clocks, the notion of passing time was fairly fluid and 'midnight' in the records probably represents a guess or a generalisation, if the word is not being used as a metaphor for the heart of darkness.

Nor should we be thrown by Katharine's reference to fairies. Belief in these preternatural beings was widespread (indeed almost universal), throughout Europe during the whole of the early modern period, and so Katharine's attempting to explain thus her sight of people in a dance (always supposing she actually had seen something of the kind, of course), would not necessarily have struck her interrogators as fanciful or mendacious, since they would have been fully conscious of (and some perhaps even shared) the immense range of communal beliefs in fairies and fairy-habits. This does not mean to say they would have approved of them – ministers were keen, officially at least, to excise and obliterate these 'superstitions', although history shows they were not successful – and neither does it entitle us to think they would have heard the evidence communicated to them with twenty-first-century ears or apprehension. Katharine's evidence (and indeed that of Jean Lilburne), therefore needs very careful attention, partly because our record of it is incomplete and partly because it stems from and is being delivered to sensibilities and understandings altogether different from our own.

Katharine thus seems to have become a victim of Jean's original testimony and Elizabeth was set to become another. Jean insisted that she and Elizabeth be confronted in the presence of the interrogators, despite their reservations and objections, and so shrill was she on this point that eventually they gave in. But first she said she wanted to retract one of her previous statements, namely, that Elizabeth was a witch. Everything else, she said, was true but not that. The interrogators were very surprised, 'seing about less than half ane hour immediatlie befoir sche constantlie deponit befoir thame that all sche said of the said Elspet Jemesoune, sche wald say it in her face', and the minister tried to cover the moment with a joke (so the record explicitly says), by asking her what she would do if Elizabeth's attendant-demon were more powerful than her own and prevented her from speaking during the confrontation. Jean replied they would not stop her from telling the truth and then, pressed by the interrogators to explain why she had suddenly changed her mind about Elizabeth, admitted that Elizabeth's husband (Alexander Falconer) had threatened to remove lumps of flesh from her every day if she continued to accuse his wife of being a witch. The magistrates assured Jean of their protection against such violence, which seems to have given her courage, for she then fell to her knees and, in front of Elizabeth herself, reaffirmed what she had formerly said of her – that Elizabeth had taken part in the midnight dancing and that it was at her request the Devil performed his act of malevolent magic.

Elizabeth angrily suggested they put Jean to the torture, 'and then sche will deny'; but the magistrates grimly answered that if they put *her* to the torture, she might be as ready to confess. An impasse had been reached. Jean, however, stuck to this version of her evidence 'both in prisone and in jugement; and at the fyre, the tow being about hir neck, quhen sche was besocht then to revok quhatever lay [lie] sche had maid upoun hir conscience, sche gave out that all was trew quhat sche had deponed'. Things therefore looked black for Elizabeth. She had been denounced as a witch by a confessing witch and narrowly escaped being accused by a second woman who was later executed as a witch. These two facts alone constituted what Del Rio would have classified as serious *indicia*, pieces of circumstantial evidence sufficient to give rise to more than suspicion, even if they provided less than absolute proof. Another, though lesser *indicium*, was her behaviour which was noted by some of the witnesses. Several of them, said her indictment, had on various occasions and in different places seen her tottering and collapsing, 'especiallie the tyme that Megg Kennedie the witch was brunt'. Elizabeth explained she was subject to colic. 'But what made you stand on your head?' she was asked. 'I didn't,' she replied, 'but sometimes the pain was so great that it made me sink to my knees and double over so that the top of my head was pressed to the ground', a detail which speaks for the authenticity of what she was saying, since it is observable that many traumatised children, for example, when suffering pain and stress seek to press their forehead against a solid object such as a wall or the floor in what appears to be an automatic and instinctive reaction. It does not seem to have been her physical symptoms in themselves, however odd, that raised suspicion so much as the fact that *she* was exhibiting them – could they (people may have thought) be signs of diabolical possession which was known to distort the body into unusual shapes? – and that Elizabeth was behaving so at the very time a friend or neighbour with whom she was known to have kept frequent company was being garrotted and burned as a witch?

Elizabeth originally faced sixteen charges altogether, however one is crossed through and we may presume it was withdrawn. But it is worth a few words further. About three years before her arrest and trial, without any invitation Elizabeth went to the house of Sir John Hamilton of Grange and there saw the family's wet-nurse giving suck to Sir John's child. Elizabeth asked a few general questions about the baby and the nurse then allowed her to hold it ('it' because the record gives no indication of the child's gender). Elizabeth noticed that the baby had an amulet round its neck – a common practice of the time, intended to ward off evil, especially the effects of the evil eye – removed it, and 'thereftir opening hir breist put her pape in the babeis mouth, quha lay therat souking hir ane lang space'. Unfortunately thereafter the child refused to suck from its wet-nurse or anyone else, contracted some kind of illness, and died, all of which the article attributed to Elizabeth's 'sorcirie and witchcraft', using the emotive word 'murdered' to describe the infant's death. The tenor of the charge is curiously reminiscent of that laid against Katharine Key in 1653. There, too, the accusation came to nothing, but one is intrigued to note that Sir John Hamilton of Grange was one of the four judges who were commissioned to preside over Elizabeth's trial, and a number of questions immediately suggest themselves. Was it at his instance that the charge was struck out? If so, why did he not believe Elizabeth was responsible? Or did he believe she was, but realised that the charge could not be proved because the principal witness would have been the wet-nurse whom the article suggested was 'simple', that is, stupid or even half-witted? What was the part played by the other three judges in having the charge dismissed? Did Sir John authorise his child's wearing of an amulet (in which case we might assume he had some personal faith in the efficacity of magic); or was this someone else's idea, the wet-nurse perhaps (in which case did Sir John approve, was he indifferent, did he not know?). It is innumerable details such as these which we lack but which were known to the participants in witchcraft cases, whose absence from the record makes reliable interpretation of these cases by us an attempt fraught with difficulty and demands that we take care before jumping to any conclusions.

The excision of this charge left fifteen others, of which one accused her of having been 'thir mony yeiris bygane' a common sorcerer and notorious witch who made and kept trysts with the Devil and other witches, practising harmful magic to the detriment of anyone who crossed her or against whom she entertained malice or evil will. Such general summarising charges were often made against Scottish suspect witches and usually form (as here) the concluding paragraph of their indictment. But Elizabeth will not have helped herself by an incident which happened about eight years previously. Henry Gray rebuked his wife, Kate Scott, for keeping company with Meg Kennedy, a witch. Kate retorted that Meg was no witch and she herself did not believe that witches existed – an interesting and unusual expression of doubt, perhaps exaggerated, though, by her wish to defend the reputation of one of her female friends. Elizabeth, however, interjected saying that she could take the hand of those who had been ridden by the Devil (that is, had had sexual intercourse with him), within the last twenty-four hours, a foolish boast since it implied she had information about practising witches, which she had not reported to the relevant authorities, and at worst that she herself was their associate, as indeed Jean Lilburne had claimed in her denunciation. But her boast may have been true in part. On 23 August 1624, only a few weeks before the trial, Jean Henderson testified to the judges that she had once had a sick cow and had told Elizabeth about it. Elizabeth recommended that Jean consult Marion MacCallaw and ask her to charm the cow. This Jean did. Marion came but, after examining the cow, said she had never seen an illness like it and that she would not attempt her magical cure. 'Thereftir', we are told, 'the kow deyid'. Clearly, then, Elizabeth knew, or at least knew of, one magical practitioner and so to this extent her claim to know local witches was true enough.

Now, it is worth our asking why Jean Lilburne named Elizabeth in the first place. The answer has nothing to do with torture or browbeating. It is to be found in one of the other charges brought against Elizabeth. About eight years previously, Elspeth Kirkcaldy sold some meal to Elizabeth and received in payment a gold coin which appeared to have been tampered with, because it was lighter in weight than it should have been. So Elspeth sent the coin back; whereupon Elizabeth lost her temper and told Elspeth she hoped her meal would never do her good. Not long after, a hundred merks' worth of meal vanished from the mill and the two women remained at loggerheads, since Elspeth suspected the meal had disappeared because of witchcraft. Elspeth and her husband then moved house and changed occupation. They set themselves up as brewsters and did rather well until

Elizabeth 'propynit hir with ane new skellie', that is, gave her a new cup; after which everything went wrong again. Having been told by John Vicar that Jean Lilburne was saying she was indeed the victim of witchcraft, Elspeth then sought Jean out and received confirmation that her misfortunes stemmed from the malevolent magic of Elizabeth Forgeston, Janet Forgeston and Elizabeth Jameson. Perhaps mistrustful of someone who may have had the reputation of being a witch herself, Elspeth brought in the local schoolmaster, David Adinston, but Jean repeated her accusation in front of him and continued to stand by it until her own death at the stake.

Jean's motives may appear to be suspicious, presenting us with the possibility that relations between the two women were hostile. Still, we do not know what was their previous relationship, of course, and so it may be that Jean named Elizabeth because Elspeth Kirkcaldy and her husband, who certainly did have personal animus against Elizabeth, fed Jean with the name and, in effect, merely asked Jean to confirm what they thought they already knew. Elizabeth's reputation may have suggested her as an obvious candidate for naming, along with the two Forgestons; or Jean may have mentioned Elizabeth and the others at a venture, extemporising, so to speak, at the end of a magic ritual intended to expose the guilty party. There were many such rituals. Very often they involved a set of names, perhaps written down on paper, and an object which was supposed to select or point to the name of the culprit. Again, in the absence of details known to the participants, we can only review possibilities; but if we do, we should take into account as wide a range of possibilities as we can, rather than pick one which chimes with our own predilections.

Jean's naming Elizabeth as a witch seems to have acted as a trigger which set in train a collection of adverse evidence which had been lying dormant in the community for at least eight years and perhaps longer; and on 18 March 1624 a warrant was issued against her. As she was pregnant at the time, it was decided that her trial (if any, of course) would not be held until after her child was delivered. Her husband, Alexander Falconer, posted the enormous sum of £500 as caution (bail), and it is likely that in late March or early April Elizabeth gave birth, for a second commission to try her for witchcraft was issued on 17 April, and from then until the trial itself in September the local officials ferreted and recorded.

Some of the charges they uncovered, we have already discussed. The others may be divided for convenience into two groups: those (by far the larger number), which accuse Elizabeth of causing some kind of financial loss to the victims of her alleged malice, and those involving a variety of magical operations commonly associated with witches – illness, death, failure of breast-milk, raising storms, causing impotence, and shape-changing. Many of these instances are collected together under a single item of the indictment. Thus, for example, John Cassells and his wife Marion Harper deponed to the court that about five years previously Elizabeth and Marion had exchanged harsh words over some cloth, and within a fortnight Elizabeth said that Marion should be laid low in spite of her fine clothes. Whereupon Marion went weeping to Marion Waugh who, however, refused to agree to testify against Elizabeth. Not long afterwards, John Cassells, a fisher-man, was invited by Elizabeth's husband to have a drink with him at home. After much hesitation, he went. Marion, needless to say, was not in the least pleased and when John returned she 'miscallit him griev-ouslie'. That same night, her breast-milk dried up and never returned. Moreover, when John went back to sea, he suffered more than one storm and eventually lost his boat, though the actual loss took place in fair weather.

Thereafter he could never make a living. For example, one day he brought home some fish, and Elizabeth came and asked if she might have some to taste; but although he gave her a few small cod, he got no money for the rest – even after he had sold some to John Paterson's wife she sent them back again – and when Marion complained to Margaret Watt that, work as he might, her husband could not put food on the table for the children, Margaret told her she had heard Elizabeth say, 'John Cassills is in ane evill estate now, bot he sal be in worse'. So indeed he was: for perhaps six weeks before the trial, Marion gave Elizabeth's daughter twenty pence to pay for a mutchkin [about ¾ pint] of wine which she and John then drank; but thereafter they were unable to have sexual intercourse, and John found himself forced to get out of bed and lie on top of the salt-chest.

It would be easy to offer rationalisations for this mish-mash of accusations. Clearly John Cassells was less hostile to Elizabeth than was his wife, and one may wonder whether the loss of intercourse and the need to sleep elsewhere than in the marital bed owed more to Marion's bad temper at her husband's failure to prosecute the feuds with Elizabeth more vigorously than to occult forces emanating from Elizabeth's malice. Nevertheless, we have already seen more than enough evidence of how misleading it can be to speculate too freely in the absence of detailed knowledge of the people and the continuous circumstances involved in any of these charges; so it will be more prudent simply to note that someone who acquired a reputation of being a magical operator inevitably ran the risk of having relationships with neighbours, friends or clients interpreted along hostile lines relating to magic should those relationships turn sour at any future date.

Complaints that Elizabeth had caused people to lose their source of income represent a majority of the reasons advanced against her. Richard Kers, her next-door neighbour, found her in his brewhouse one evening and very soon afterwards he lost two brewings, and continued so to fail in his trade that he was forced to give it up. His wife, too, fell sick and died a fortnight later. As if this were not enough, the incident was repeated some time later, after Richard had married again. Discovering Elizabeth in his brewhouse late at night, Richard was very angry and would have hit her had his wife not restrained him. Elizabeth spoke soothingly, promising never to be found so again; but the moment she was beyond his reach, she said she would make him die a beggar and, sure enough, his brewing business failed for a second time in his life.

Thomas Paterson's brewing went the same way as Richard's and so too, almost, did his wife. She became very ill and seemed to be at death's door until she sent for Elizabeth and asked her three times to give her back her health ('chargeing hir in the name of God secreitlie in hir mynd'); whereupon she recovered with extraordinary speed.

Now, at some point – the record does not make it clear exactly when – Elizabeth must have been arrested and put in prison. Whether this was upon complaints of witchcraft or for some other reason, we do not know. But whatever the cause, she was released, because we are told that 'efter sche was suffered to come out of ward', she bought a sack of malt from Thomas and tried to borrow his horse to carry it to the mill. Thomas demurred, saying his horse was lame, but Elizabeth was importunate and eventually Thomas lent her another horse which was weak in the legs but had good eyesight. The inevitable (one might be led to guess) happened, however, and when Elizabeth returned the horse it was blind in both eyes but sound in all four legs. Alexander Glen also lost his brewing, John Stevenson a horse, Robert Love a cow, John Hay his entire means of earning a living, and Thomas Gleg his ox and his kiln. Each of these losses was alleged to have happened after the principal or his wife or both had quarrelled with Elizabeth – a quarrel which the documents represent as starting with her: but since they are recording evidence from hostile sources, the bias is scarcely surprising. Thomas Gleg, for example, had taken Elizabeth to court to recover a debt, whereas Elizabeth maintained he had foisted a false debt upon her, and without any further details in the case we have no sure means of telling whether Thomas or she was in the right.

This uncertainty bedevills our interpretation of the relationships between most witches and their accusers. The theme of quarrel followed by magical retribution in one form or another (usually out of all proportion to the perceived or alleged offence), is common to the great majority of witchcraft cases throughout Europe, and yet it is noticeable that relations between the suspect witch and her or his neighbours are very much more complex than this clichéd pattern might suggest. For example, John Cassells and his wife, despite the high words and threats exchanged with Elizabeth and the losses apparently consequent upon those threats, continued to do business with her.

It might be argued, of course, that they did so from fear of the consequences if they did not. So let us take the case of William Gibb, a fisherman in Bo'ness, who testified against Elizabeth at her trial. About four years previously, he went out at midnight to fish and his daughter-in-law, Jean Woodrup, a young girl of twelve, came and sat at the pier-head to await his return. While Jean was waiting there, Elizabeth came to the pier-head and engaged her in conversation. Jean told her she had come to buy fish when William got back, but Elizabeth replied, 'Willie will sell no fishe this nyt', and then suddenly vanished from sight, returning soon afterwards in the likeness of a grey cat. At this point, 'the air began to altir, the sky darkned with blak clouds round about, and ane horrible tempest of wind arraised'. No sooner had the storm struck than William himself became paralysed, unable to move or speak – something which had never happened to him before. Jean immediately rushed home to tell her mother (Elspeth Kers, William's wife) what had happened, shrieking so loudly that she woke the neighbours. Elspeth at first seemed incapable of doing anything, but then one of her neighbours, Marion Gibb, came in and urged her forcefully to pull herself together. 'I command thee, woman, in the name of God, to arryse and go seik thy husband'. The tide was now coming in. Elspeth waded out to the salmon-traps which had been set in the tideway and there found William still standing 'nather hable to speik or move out of his place'. Gripping hold of him, Elspeth managed to drag him back to dry land where he seems to have regained his powers of speech and movement.

All this, says the indictment, was done by 'the said Elizabeth, hir devillirie and witchcraft', and yet a note in the margin observes that while William avowed the truth of his sudden sickness, he could not be prevailed on to swear that Elizabeth was the cause. The judges seem to have been puzzled by this and asked Elizabeth if there was any ill will between her and William. She answered, not to her knowledge, and both William and Elspeth said the same. The judges, however, remarked that this argued in favour of their testimony being true, for if there were no ill-will, there was no cause for them to manufacture a lie; and their refusal to swear it was Elizabeth who had bewitched William at that time was taken by the judges as further proof of his and Elspeth's sincerity. There is also the possibility that some people, at least, were nervous of Elizabeth's violent temper. When Richard Ewing, a butcher in Bo'ness, refused to sell her meat from his stall for the low price she was offering him, for example, she pretended she wanted to whisper something in his ear and then, when he came close, bit it until it bled. Elizabeth's version of this incident was that when she came to buy meat Richard, observing that her husband had been away at sea for rather a long time, tried to make a pass at her; so she smacked his face and the nail on her little finger, 'being sumwhat long', scratched his ear, and because he was rather flushed he bled more easily.

But William and Elspeth were not the only people unwilling to take their oath that Elizabeth was guilty of witchcraft. Richard Kers 'being askit by the juges if he wold swear that [Elizabeth] was the cause of all his crossis and lossis... ansuerit, not for all the world'. He indeed, like William, was willing to swear to the truth of his problems, 'and withall protested that this long tyme he hes had in his hert a rooted suspicion that sche was not good, bot would not justefie it by his oath'. Why would he not? Perhaps he (and the others) had genuine doubts that Elizabeth was a witch; perhaps he believed she was, but was too afraid to risk crossing her; perhaps he thought she was a witch, but did not think it was she who had actually been responsible for his troubles. His long suspicion that 'she was not good' argues against his being a sceptic. It may be that when he heard she had been arrested and that various people were testifying against her, he cast in his two penn'orth partly as a mark of solidarity with his neighbours, partly to test his suspicions of her guilt. Whatever the truth, people's hesitations to take an oath that she was the witch who had caused their problems shows that there is no easy formula (quarrel = disaster = accusation of witchcraft = judicial proof thereof) wherewith one may build a single theory to explain why such accusations occurred.

Earlier I artificially divided the charges against Elizabeth into two groups. The first related to her causing loss of goods or income. Some of the second can be seen in the case involving William Gibb. Raising storms was a traditional malefice attributed to witches; so was their ability to change shape. John Rannale and his wife, Margaret Mitchell, both deponed they had heard young John Howie swear that once, while he and Elizabeth were returning to Bo'ness from Linlithgow, she asked him to carry her plaids and suddenly vanished away, after which he saw nothing but a hare running up and along the hills. The boy walked for about half a mile 'in great feir and pirplexitie of mynd', and then Elizabeth reappeared in her own shape, disappeared once more, and John saw the hare again. Having arrived in Bo'ness, he reported what he had seen, but shortly afterwards fell sick and eventually died, 'and so was crewallie murdreit and slane be the said Elizabeth, hir sorcirie and witchcraft'. Raising storms, shape-changing, causing impotence, drying up breast-milk, possessing the evil eye, having the ability to lift as well as inflict bewitchment, not to mention dancing with the Devil – how many of these were attributed to Elizabeth because, genuine afflictions and experiences though they may have been for her neighbours, they were the kind of thing witches were supposed to be able to do?

Elspeth Kirkcaldy makes a tantalising remark. In response to her loss of brewing, which forced her husband to leave the district and look for work elsewhere, she says she would never have attributed her troubles to Elizabeth 'if Jeane Lilburne befoir hir convictioun and executioun in presens of famous [respectable] witnesses had not delaitit hir, with Elspeth and Jonet Fergusone, be their sorcirie and witchcraft to have bene the instrumentis of the wrak of hir and hir husband'. So was it merely the appearance of Elizabeth's name in Jean's testimony which led to her arrest and interrogation?

One should not jump to conclusions. Janet Dunbar was arrested in Culross on charges of witchcraft and maintained (having been told so by her personal spirit 'Peter') that Elizabeth was responsible for bewitching Richard Ewing, a claim she stood by right up to her own execution. Elizabeth had therefore been denounced by *two* confessing witches. Whether they had ever been brought together and so had an opportunity to exchange names (wittingly or not), we do not know; but their testimony – which may have been offered independently on different occasions and in different places – would certainly have looked bad for Elizabeth. So too would her acquaintance or friendship with Jean and another convicted witch, Meg Kennedy. She also knew of Marion MacCallow, a charmer of cattle, and may have been friendly with her, in which case her keeping company with known magical operators would have looked that much worse. We have also seen that Elizabeth was neither ashamed of such acquaintance nor reticent about it, boasting openly at one point that she could 'put her hand on' those who had lain with the Devil during the past twenty-four hours. If she was merely a woman who liked to pretend she knew more than she did, or who took an open delight in keeping louche company, her trial in September would have sobered her excitement and revealed the grave suspicions her neighbours had been entertaining for nearly a decade. To some extent, then, she had little cause to complain at her arrest, since her behaviour had invited it to happen sooner or later.

Four judges had commission to preside over her trial. Sir John Hamilton of Grange, whose name was mentioned in the item struck from her dittay (indictment), had been appointed Sheriff of Linlithgow very recently, on 25 August. The year 1624 was busy for him. On 5 February he received a commission to try Elspeth Paris and her husband for witchcraft; on 18 March, another to try Jean Lilburne and Christian Hay from Bo'ness, Elspeth Ferguson, William Falconer, Marion Simson, and Elizabeth herself, all for witchcraft; on 30 March, a third to try Katharine Blair, Janet Dunbar and Isobel Coutts, all from Bo'ness; and a fourth on 17 April to try Elizabeth who had been pregnant and near her time at the end of March. Clearly there was something of a flurry of witch-trials in the area, since six of the eleven people are known to have come from Bo'ness and the likelihood seems to be that most were originally named and implicated by Jean Lilburne. Walter Cornwall of Bonhard and John Drummond of Woodcockdale had been appointed justices of peace for the shire of Linlithgow on 20 August 1623 and they, along with Sir John Hamilton of Bearcroft, received commissions to sit with Sir John Hamilton of Grange in March and April 1624 to try this same group of local witches.

The assize (jury) consisted of fifteen men (the usual number), drawn partly from Bo'ness and the immediate neighbourhood and partly from further afield (the usual arrangement), thereby providing a mixture of those who knew well both the accused persons and the local circumstances, and those who did not. When it came to hearing the evidence Elizabeth, like every accused person in a Scottish court, had the right to object to a witness on the grounds that he or she was likely to be biased against her, and when the witnesses took the oath, they had to swear they bore no malice against the panel (accused); indeed, during Elizabeth's trial, the judges were careful to question more than one witness on this very point. So the conduct of the trial, as in the majority of Scottish trials for witchcraft, was intended to demonstrate a degree of fairness to the person in the dock, so that justice might be seen to be done in deed as well as in appearance. Interestingly enough, in Elizabeth's case, the judges also removed from consideration the item in her dittay which described her as boasting she could identify local witches, declaring the point 'nawayis relevant to pass to ane assyse [jury] as witchcraft', by which they clearly meant that her possible ability to identify witches was not an act of witchcraft in itself.

Once the witnesses had been heard, the assize retired to elect its chancellor (foreman), who would deliver the verdict in court, and to consider the evidence which had been laid before it. We do not have any record of its deliberations in Elizabeth's case, but from other witchcraft trials we know that each point of the dittay would have been debated separately and a vote taken. The opinions of the assizors might therefore vary considerably from item to item. They could acquit the panel entirely on one point while unanimously finding her or him guilty of another. On most points, however, their judgement was divided and so each item would be marked *clenged* (acquitted) or *fylit* (found guilty) according to a majority verdict. To arrive at a final verdict on the whole dittay, these separate judgements were added up, and the panel was condemned or acquitted according to the majority balance produced therefrom.

The charges against Elizabeth involved dancing with the Devil and other witches, causing people loss of property and income, laying on and taking off bewitchment, causing illness to people and death to animals, drying up breast-milk, raising storms, shape-changing, and inducing impotence, not to mention the catch-all article which related to her having been a witch for many years past – a gallimaufry of malefices which both could have been and often was alleged of witches throughout the early modern period. The assize came to its verdict and filed back into the court-room. Their deliberations would not have taken very long. Scottish trials tended to be fairly short. Their verdict was given by the chancellor. 'The haill pirsonis of assyse, all in one voice, clengis Elspeth Jamesoun of the haill poynts contenit in hir dittay' – a unanimous declaration of 'not guilty'.

What does this verdict mean? We must not rush to assume that 'not guilty' indicates the assizors did not believe Elizabeth was a witch at all. The verdict could mean that, of course, but it could also mean they were not convinced on the evidence laid before them that Elizabeth had committed the acts of malefice alleged against her. This is a long way from saying, 'she is not a witch', for we need to bear in mind our earlier discussion of the way charges of witchcraft often surfaced in Scottish society: insults flung against a woman, frequently during the course of a quarrel or as the result of bad blood, which were then made the object of a complaint in front of a kirk session. Calling a woman 'whore' or 'thief' or 'witch', I suggested, was more likely to be damagingly effective if the community could see there might be at least some truth underlying the insult, and we can detect one or two signs of this in the evidence against Elizabeth. Jean Grinlaw shouted at Elizabeth's daughter, telling her, 'Go home and tell your hussie [woman of bad character] the Devill be in hir eye'; and Richard Ewing, in despair at losing his income as a result of what he suspected was Elizabeth's hostile magic, said directly to her, 'Good wyfe, ye have more power than God has given you to tak away my goods. I charge you in the name of God to give me thame bak agane and to do me no more wrong'. The assize may have acquitted Elizabeth of being the actual cause of harm to these people, but her alleged victims had clearly believed there was sufficient evidence in her appearance (the evil eye) and in her disposition to warrant calling her a witch. It was her misfortune, perhaps, that she ended in front of a criminal court; but it could equally well have been simple good luck which produced a verdict in her favour.

AFTERWORD

If there was one thing people found difficult about the recognition of witches, it was the ever-present realisation, sometimes overt but usually tacit, that appearances are deceptive. God had created a universe one could see and readily apprehend. There was the earth, above it were the seven planets, and beyond them was the great zone of the fixed stars. Everything he had created was, in one sense, available to the eye. But that one sense was not enough; for behind visible reality lay other realities – realm after realm of angels, spirits, ghosts, elementals, non-human entities of all kinds, Heaven itself, Hell, Purgatory, Limbo – all known to exist because they made their existence known to human beings again and again, usually without warning, while visions and signs and portents crossed the skies or appeared in physical objects, apparently out of nowhere. People lived in a constant state of subliminal awareness that the material universe was little more than a flimsy veil concealing who knew how many universes, each of them faintly resembling and yet quite unlike that which God had created to house their bodies, just as the heavenly Jerusalem described in the *Apocalypse* reminded them of an earthly city, and yet was different from any they knew in every respect. Nothing, then, was as it seemed to be.

Now, living in a world of appearances must have had its difficulties as well as its consolations. It would have been a source of comfort on the one hand to have had available those who could see into and interpret the future, recognise the meaning of signs, mediate between this world and the others, and manipulate the hidden laws of nature to produce benefits otherwise unattainable; while on the other, it would have been a source of distress and fear to know that there existed those who were prepared and able to summon non-human entities for the purpose of working harm, and who were willing to ally themselves with those unseen forces whose purpose was to overturn the world's order into chaos and drag every human being through the veil into a perpetual state of terror and exquisite pain. Identifying the latter was thus not only desirable, it was essential. But it was not easy, for they generally looked and sounded and behaved like everyone else. It was only when their secret allegiances were uncovered that the rest of the community could feel it was safe (although perhaps just for the moment), from a lethal intrusion into their lives by forces they knew were stronger than they were, and deadly. Whatever method of identification worked, or appeared to work, was therefore a Godsend, almost literally; and whatever doubts anyone may have had about the efficacity of any individual test were outweighed by the conviction that any means whereby the agents of evil might be detected, however flawed, were surely better than none.

Notes

Bibliographic Notice

List of Illustrations

Index

NOTES

1　All translations are the author's.
2　De Lancre uses the masculine form of the word, but he is clearly following Latin usage in which a masculine adjective or noun may be inclusive of the feminine.
3　Terence Cave has drawn attention to this. See his *Pré-histoires: Textes troublées au seuil de la modernité* (Librairie Droz, Geneva, 1999), 75–76.
4　J. Spottiswoode, *The History of the Church of Scotland*, 3 vols (London, 1851), 2.448.
5　R. Gardiner, *Englands Grievance Discovered in Relation to the Coal Trade* (London, 1655), 114.
6　*Enemies of God* (Blackwell, Oxford, 1983), 111.
7　Scots quotations have been changed in places into modern English for clarity.

BIBLIOGRAPHICAL NOTICE

Much of the material used in this book comes either from manuscript sources, or from early modern authors not yet translated into English. Specific bibliography relating to the authors, people and subject matter discussed here is therefore somewhat limited. Abbreviations used in the text are as follows: *JC* = Records of the High Court of Justiciary in Edinburgh; *CH* = Records of the Scottish kirk and presbytery sessions; *RPC* = Records of the Privy Council of Scotland.

On Martín Del Rio there is very little in English apart from my own edited translation of his *Disquisitiones Magicae* under the title *Martín Del Rio: Investigations into Magic* (Manchester, Manchester University Press, 2001). This contains a preliminary essay on both Del Rio himself and a summary of his work. On Pierre de Lancre, see M.M. McGowan, 'Pierre de Lancre's *Tableau de l'inconstance des mauvais anges et demons*', in S. Anglo (ed.), *The Damn'd Art* (London, Routledge and Kegan Paul, 1977), Chapter 8; S. Houdard, *Les sciences du diable: quatre discours sur la sorcellerie* (Paris, Etudes du Cerf, 1992), Chapter 4; G.S. Williams, *Defining Dominion: The Discourses of Magic and Witchcraft in Early Modern France and Germany* (Ann Arbor, University of Michigan, 1999), Chapter 5; F. Bordes, *Sorciers et sorcières: procès de sorcellerie en Gascogne et Pays Basque* (Toulouse, Editions Privat, 1999), Part 2, Chapter 1. On Battista Codronchi, see W. Schleiner, *Medical Ethics in the Renaissance* (Washington, Georgetown University Press, 1995), Chapter 4. On the evil eye, see F. Salmon & M. Cabré, 'Fascinating women: the evil eye in medical Scholasticism', in R. French, J. Arrizabalaga, A. Cunningham & L. García-Ballester (eds), *Medicine from the Black Death to the French Disease* (Ashgate, 1998), 53–84; F. Bowie, *The Anthropology of Religion* (Oxford, Blackwell, 2000), Chapter 8. On possession, see S. Clark, *Thinking With Demons*, (Oxford, Clarendon Press, 1997), Chapters 26–28; W. Frijhoff, 'Sorcellerie et possession du Moyen Age aux Lumières', *Revue d'histoire ecclésiastique* 95 (2000), 112–42. On Kincaid, see S.W. MacDonald, 'The Devil's mark and the witch-prickers of Scotland', *Journal of the Royal Society of Medicine* 90 (1997), 507–11; more generally, B.P. Levack, 'The great Scottish witch-hunt of 1661–1662', *Journal of British Studies* 20 (1980), 90–108. On swimming, see R. Zguta, 'The ordeal by water (swimming of witches) in the East Slavic world', *Slavic Review* 36 (1977), 220–30.

LIST OF ILLUSTRATIONS

Illustrations courtesy of the author unless otherwise stated.

1 Instructing Church and State in the ways of witchcraft.
2 Title-page to Martín Del Rio's *Disquisitiones Magicae*.
3 Satan presiding at the Sabbat.
4 Jan Ziarnko's illustration of a witches' Sabbat.
5 A male witch is interrogated and hanged.
6 Physician studying a specimen of urine.
7 An example of the written pact between a priest and the Devil.
8 The effects of the evil eye.
9 Title-page to Battista Codronchi's *De morbis veneficis*.
10 Cotton Mather.
11 A priest exorcising a demon from a possessed woman.
12 Pittenweem in 1877. By permission of the University Library, St Andrews University, Scotland.
13 Kirk session entry relating to witches in Pittenweem, 29 May 1704. By permission of the National Archives of Scotland.
14 Satan marking a male witch.
15 The sieve and shears.
16 Swimming a witch.
17 A male and a female witch raising a storm at sea.
18 Christian Ulrich Grupen, *Observatio iuris criminalis de applicatione tormentorum* (Hanover, 1754).

INDEX

DATE DUE